# PLAY + LEARN
## ACTIVITIES FOR BABIES

### 65 SIMPLE WAYS
to Promote Growth & Development
from Birth to Two Years Old

## HANNAH FATHI
creator of BABY PLAY HACKS

PAGE STREET
PUBLISHING CO.

PAGE STREET
PUBLISHING CO.

Copyright © 2021 Hannah Fathi

First published in 2021 by
Page Street Publishing Co.
27 Congress Street, Suite 105
Salem, MA 01970
www.pagestreetpublishing.com

Distributed by Macmillan, sales in Canada by The Canadian Manda Group.

25   24   23   22   21      1   2   3   4   5

ISBN-13: 978-1-64567-398-9
ISBN-10: 1-64567-398-7

Library of Congress Control Number: 2021931364

Cover and book design by Rosie Stewart for Page Street Publishing Co.
Photography by Hannah Fathi

Printed and bound in China

Page Street Publishing protects our planet by donating to nonprofits like The Trustees,
which focuses on local land conservation.

TO MY CHILDREN, WHO WERE INTEGRAL,
YET OFTEN HINDRANCES, TO THE WRITING
OF THIS BOOK.

# CONTENTS

# INTRODUCTION

We know babies and young toddlers eat, sleep and cry. But how do they play? How can you develop their language and motor skills, emotional intelligence, creativity and problem-solving abilities and occupy them all day? In this book, you will find easy ways to help your child learn and grow through play—without expensive toys and subscription services.

Babies need quality face-to-face interactions, time playing on the floor and opportunities to use their bodies and minds, but coming up with ways to play can feel daunting when you are tied up with diapers, feedings and nap schedules. I've been there! When my first child was a baby, I searched for play ideas on the Internet for hours, but I couldn't find enough ideas that were engaging and safe to keep her occupied. I began Baby Play Hacks to share the baby play ideas I invented, and I wrote this book as a way to provide parents and caregivers with simple, engaging and inexpensive play ideas from birth through toddlerhood. Your home is a treasure trove of play elements, from recycled materials and craft supplies to socks and kitchen utensils. The activities and do-it-yourself toys in this book utilize items you already have in order to create enriching experiences for your child. Don't buy expensive, bulky toys that will be used sparingly and then become clutter when your child can learn and have a blast with items like cardboard boxes that require minimal preparation.

Each activity is inspired by Montessori and holistic learning principles and includes tips to play in multiple ways that maximize early language, motor and social skill development. While some projects are geared toward infants—like the Tummy Time Stand (page 14)—and some toward older babies and toddlers—like the Wipeable Car Play Mat (page 26)—they can all be used in a variety of ways and adapted for a range of ages and stages. Projects are divided into chapters by type of play and the skills they promote, like "Dexterity- and Coordination-Building Play" (page 65) and "Engaging Sensory Play" (page 91). Refer to the icons at the top of each project to see the more specific skills it will help develop—such as matching, counting and communicating—as well as the primary age range the project is ideal for. You can also flip to the Project Recommendations by Age (page 175) and Project Index by Skill (page 176) to quickly select a project that meets your child's needs.

With these sixty-five projects, your child will investigate, imagine, move and explore, building their brain from the very beginning. Create object-permanence toys, sensory bottles, shakers, puzzles and more for your baby or toddler to explore—without breaking the bank!

*Hannah Fathi*

A NOTE ABOUT SUPERVISION: These projects assume close and constant supervision by a responsible adult. You know your child best—any projects that include options involving small parts should be used at your best discretion by a child who no longer mouths nonfood objects. The crafts in this book are intended to be made by an adult and involve sharp tools and hot glue, so create carefully.

# TIPS FOR BABY AND TODDLER PLAYTIME

Baby and toddler play can feel intimidating—babies and toddlers fall over frequently when learning to move, mouth objects and have short attention spans. Set up your environment for their success with the following suggestions.

## CREATE A "YES SPACE"

Set aside a corner of your home—whether in your living room, a bedroom or playroom—that is safe for your child. This should be an area where you can say yes to anything they want to explore. Begin with a soft surface for play, like a water-resistant play mat or washable rug with a nonslip underlay. Section the area off and remove any loose cords, sharp or breakable objects or choking hazards.

## INVITE PLAY

Your child's play environment shapes their learning—a chaotic and unorganized play space can make focusing on one task challenging, and conditions without enough stimulation can lead to boredom.[1] One way to set up your play space is to set out some small baskets or make room on a low bookshelf—but watch those corners!—and add a few toys at a time.

Rotate the toys, switching items out as your child loses interest in the items available—every three to seven days for a baby or toddler, or as needed. Often, the more items that are on display—especially if they are in big bins and not visible or easily accessible—the less your child will play.[1] Include toys that are primarily open-ended rather than battery-operated with flashing lights and lots of buttons. Open-ended toys are toys that inspire creativity and learning and can be used in multiple ways, often throughout childhood, reducing the need to replace toys and buy new items.[2] Some examples include blocks, animal figurines, dolls, toy food, balls, scarves and bowls. Supplement your toy collection with activities from this book!

## ENCOURAGE INDEPENDENCE

Playing with your child is beneficial—children model behavior and need face-to-face interaction with others.[3] There is no magic amount of time that you must play with your child, but dedicating at least ten minutes of attentive play per day is a great start. You can also begin encouraging independent play and modeling focus from babyhood.

Babies and toddlers typically have an attention span of two to five minutes for one task—though it may seem like your child is moving on quickly, doing so is developmentally normal.[4] Model focus for your child by paying attention when playing with them and sticking to the task at hand. Try to follow your child's cues and encourage them to take the lead. It is okay to help them, but sit back and observe periodically to give your child time to learn and react.[5]

Help your child work up to longer spans of independent play by slowly increasing the amount of time you are not directly involved in their play, or moving farther away each day for a few minutes while they play on their own.

## PROMOTE STRENGTH AND MOVEMENT

Movement fosters learning, and when babies and toddlers are able to explore the world around them, they understand and retain more information.[6] Floor time is the foundation of movement for babies, and time playing on their tummies, backs and sides leads to strength and, eventually, mobility.[7] From the very beginning, you can focus on placing your newborn on the floor to play, rather than in a bouncy chair or other restrictive container.

Tummy time is essential for strengthening your baby's neck, shoulders, arms and core, as well as preventing flat spots on their head.[8] Aim for a few minutes at a time, a few times a day, and work up to longer periods as they become stronger. For better arm position, tuck your baby's elbows in and ensure they are completely underneath baby's shoulders.[9] You can also fit tummy time into your day by laying your baby's tummy down on your chest, across or on your legs or even cradled in your arms tummy down.

## GET CREATIVE

Play doesn't need to be complicated or expensive, and less is often more for baby and toddler play. Instead of buying new toys, turn to your recycling bin as a treasure trove for activities and crafts. This book uses recycled materials for many activities, and the following items are great things to save:

- Cardboard boxes
- Shoeboxes
- Cereal boxes
- Plastic lids
- Paper towel tubes
- Toilet paper tubes
- Ice pop or craft sticks
- Plastic bottles
- Cake or pie tins
- Single socks
- Colorful straws
- Plastic cups
- Paper egg cartons
- Broken crayons
- Baby food pouches and lids

# STRENGTHENING AND ACTIVE PLAY

Your child is learning in many ways, and developing motor skills and strength is a crucial part of your little one's development. Active play and time playing on the floor in various positions will strengthen large muscle groups and hone your child's senses. Core strength is also a vital precursor for developing fine motor skills—stability leads to mobility and dexterity.[10] Prioritize time playing on the floor, as well as standing and sitting independently—freedom to move is vital for growth. The projects in this chapter, like the Tummy Time Stand (page 14), will help make tummy time endurable. They will also give you ideas for new play positions—try the Color Cap Match on page 35. Finally, this chapter's projects will encourage your child to move. Make the *Vroom! Vroom!* Box Car on page 23 and see for yourself!

# TUMMY TIME STAND

Tummy time is an important time for baby to strengthen their neck, back and shoulders and prevent flat spots on their head. This simple tummy time stand will make it easier to entertain your baby and encourage them to lift their head and push up on their arms. The wipeable pockets can hold pattern cards, photographs, unique materials or even images from magazines. High-contrast images like black stripes and circles will draw your newborn's attention—as your baby grows, try adding more colors and shapes. Bring this craft back out for your toddler and insert coloring sheets or blank paper. They can draw with dry-erase markers on the sheet protectors, then easily wipe them clean—doing so while on their tummy will continue to strengthen their wrists, arms and shoulders.

Ruler

Precision crafting knife

Cardboard

Pencil

4 clear plastic sheet protectors for 8½ x 11" (21 x 28-cm) paper

4 (8½ x 11" [21 x 28-cm]) sheets of black paper

Hot glue gun and glue

Clear packing tape

Black marker

4 (4 x 6" [10 x 15-cm]) blank index cards

1. With the ruler and precision crafting knife, measure and cut 2 (17 x 12½–inch [43 x 31–cm]) pieces of cardboard. Score one piece of cardboard in the middle lengthwise, so that it can fold without breaking. With the pencil and ruler, mark the middle of the other cardboard piece.

2. Cut the sheet protectors lengthwise so they are 6¼ x 11 inches (16 x 28 cm), removing the binder holes.

3. Cut the sheets of black paper so that they each measure 8½ x 6¼ inches (21 x 16 cm). Put 1 piece of paper into each sheet protector and slide the paper to the sealed sides.

4. Now turn the sheet protectors into 4 pockets, 2 per cardboard piece. On the lower half of each cardboard piece, hot-glue the short, sealed side of 1 sheet protector to the middle of the cardboard. The edges of the black paper and cardboard should align. Apply hot glue to the rest of the sheet protector's back and adhere it to the cardboard.

5. The second pocket will be adhered to the first pocket and the cardboard. Line up the edge of the black paper with the other edge of the cardboard—the sealed side of the sheet protector should face the middle of the cardboard. Hot-glue the loose sheet protector to the secured sheet protector and to the cardboard. You will have 2 pockets overlapped and adhered to the cardboard, and the black paper will be aligned on both sides with the cardboard. Ensure the paper is not glued and can be slid in and out of the protector. Repeat with the remaining sheet protectors on the other cardboard piece.

6. Pull the open sides of the sheet protectors to the back of the cardboard and tape them down so they are taut.

7. Fold the scored cardboard sheet and apply hot glue on top of the line drawn on the other cardboard sheet and at the top edge of the sheet. Glue the top edge and bottom edges of the folded sheet to the flat sheet to form a triangle. Hold the edges together until the glue has dried.

8. With a black marker, draw patterns on 4 blank index cards.

9. Insert the pattern cards into the clear pockets. The sheet protectors will protect the cards and images from drool and spit up during tummy time!

# SPIDER WEB TOY GRAB

As baby learns to sit and strengthens their core, they may need somewhere to sit slightly assisted. There is no need to buy seats to prop up baby–just place them in a laundry basket! Give them a fun fine motor task that encourages investigation with just string and loose parts or small toys. Make this easier or harder for baby by varying the amount of string and how much it crosses. As an extra challenge, give your toddler tongs to pick up the objects!

Laundry basket with holes

Ruler

Scissors

String

Miscellaneous toys (such as soft bath toys, teethers or blocks)

1. Find a laundry basket that has holes in the sides, like the basket pictured.

2. With the ruler and scissors, measure and cut at least 4 pieces of string that are 1 yard (1 m) or longer. Tie one end of a length of string through one of the basket's holes, then pass the string back and forth through the holes diagonally and vertically to create a web. Leave one side of the basket empty for baby to sit. Add as many pieces of string as you would like to make the challenge more or less difficult.

3. Place the toys under the string web.

4. Seat your baby on the empty side of the basket and push the basket against a wall or other surface to ensure that it will not tip backward. If needed, place soft blankets around the basket in case it tips sideways. Encourage your child to pick up the toys, and supervise closely!

# RATTLE SOCKS

Find a pair or mismatched set of baby socks to make these rattles that encourage baby to kick, walk or shake! As young babies become aware of their bodies, these rattles will help them understand that they are moving their own feet. Stretchy baby socks will fit on most older babies' feet as well, and as they learn to walk they will be motivated to make noise as they step. You can even slip these socks on your toddler's hands to make rattle mittens.

4 plastic bottle caps

Alcohol swab or nail polish remover

1 tsp uncooked rice

Hot glue gun and glue

2 baby socks

Plastic bottle

1. Wipe the labels off of four plastic bottle caps with an alcohol swab. Some labels wipe off more easily than others.

2. Add ½ teaspoon of the uncooked rice to 2 of the bottle caps.

3. Apply hot glue around the rim of the other 2 bottle caps and carefully place them on top of the rice-filled caps. Allow the glue to dry completely before lifting the rattles.

4. Stretch a baby sock over the top of a plastic bottle so that the sock is taut.

5. Apply hot glue to one side of a bottle cap rattle and glue the cap to the top of the sock, close to the toe seam. Repeat this process with the other rattle and sock and allow the glue to dry completely.

6. Put the socks on baby's feet during back playtime to encourage them to kick. Older babies and toddlers will enjoy walking, jumping and kicking with the socks on their feet. They may even like wearing them on their hands as rattle mittens. Gently hand-wash the rattle socks if needed.

2.

3.

4.

5.

# TRANSFORMING DISKS

Teach your child about metamorphosing frogs and butterflies and hatching chicks with this do-it-yourself toy that is sure to be a hit. Babies can sit and play; leaning forward to spin the disks will strengthen your baby's core and encourage them to sit upright. They can also lie down and spin the disks above them, strengthening their arms, shoulders and wrists. Let your toddler learn by spinning and watching the tadpole become a frog, the chick hatch from the egg and the caterpillar turn into a butterfly. Talk to them about what is happening in simple terms and spark their curiosity!

Pencil

Large Circle Template (page 173)

White computer paper

Scissors

1 (9 x 12" [23 x 30-cm]) sheet of stiff felt in each of the following colors: gray, white, yellow, orange, dark green and light green

Black permanent marker

1½ yards (1.5 m) string

Hot glue gun and glue

Transformation Templates (page 162)

Play gym or sturdy chair

1. To make the disks, lightly trace the Large Circle Template onto a white sheet of paper and cut it out. Then trace the circle cutout onto a 9 x 12–inch (23 x 30–cm) gray felt sheet six times with a black permanent marker. Cut the disks out with sharp scissors.

2. To attach the disks to the string, first lay 3 of the disks in a row on a work surface, spaced 1 inch (2.5 cm) apart. Lay the string over the center of the disks, with the center of the middle disk and the string aligned.

3. Apply hot glue to the 3 disks, covering the disks and gluing over the string well. Quickly place the other 3 disks over the glued disks, aligning them and sandwiching the string between each pair.

4. While the glue dries, trace the Transformation Templates onto the white paper. Cut the shapes out of the paper and then trace them onto the remaining felt. Trace the egg onto the white felt, the chick, caterpillar and butterfly body onto the yellow felt, the whole butterfly onto the orange felt and the leaf onto the dark green. To create the butterfly's back wing, trace the template again, leaving off the body of the butterfly and tracing just the wing. If desired, draw a small triangular beak on the orange felt and small eyes for the chick, frog, butterfly, caterpillar and tadpole on the gray felt.

5. To create the frog, first trace the outline of the frog template onto the dark green felt. Cut along the centerline of the template, and trace the bottom half of the frog onto the light green felt. To create the tadpole, first trace the outline of the tadpole template onto the dark green felt, then cut off the outer portion of the tail and trace the remaining portion of the tail and the body onto the light green felt.

(continued)

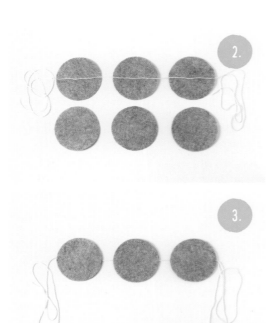

6. Cut out all the felt pieces with scissors.

7. Hot-glue the caterpillar on top of the leaf. Hot-glue the back butterfly wing behind the remaining butterfly wing and body. Hot-glue the light green portion of the frog on top of the dark green portion, aligning the body. Hot-glue the light green portion of the tadpole on top of the dark green portion, aligning the head.

8. Hot-glue the butterfly, chick and frog to the 3 gray disks. Flip the disks over. Orient the images on the backs of the disks as you would expect to see them if you were looking at them head-on. When you spin the disks, the images should be facing the correct direction. Hot-glue the leaf and caterpillar to the other side of the butterfly disk, the egg to the other side of the chick disk and the tadpole to the other side of the frog disk. If desired, hot-glue eyes and a beak onto the chick and eyes onto the frog. When you spin the disks, the images should all be oriented correctly.

9. When the glue is dry, tie the ends of the string tightly to the legs of a play gym or a sturdy chair. Baby can sit in front of the disks to spin them or lie underneath the disks to reach up and grab them. Another great way to play is to tie the ends of the string to both sides of a plastic laundry basket and have your child sit inside the basket to spin the disks. Push the basket against a wall so that it will not tip backward. Closely supervise playtime, especially if your baby is seated in front of the disks.

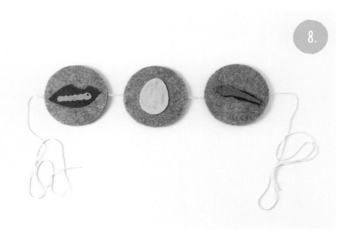

# VROOM! VROOM! BOX CAR

Imaginative play has many benefits for babies and children, improving their understanding of the world around them and encouraging exploration and curiosity.[13] Playing with a box car is a simple way to engage baby and also promote gross motor play. Your child can sit in the car while you push it, or your child can push toys around in the car. Sing "The Wheels on the Bus" while baby turns the steering wheel and talk about all the people and places you imagine passing.

Ruler

Box cutter

Large piece of flat cardboard

Large cardboard box

Hot glue gun and glue

Pencil

Clear packing tape

5 brad paper fasteners

5 paper plates

2 plastic cups

Paintbrush and nontoxic paint or crayons (optional)

1. With the ruler and box cutter, measure and cut a piece of flat cardboard that is the same size as the bottom interior of the large cardboard box. Hot-glue the cardboard inside the box to reinforce the bottom of the box car.

2. Hot-glue one of the box's short flaps to the inside of the box to reinforce the back of the car. Lightly mark the back of the box car with a pencil so you can tell the front and back apart.

3. Seal the top of the box with the packing tape. Divide the top of the box into roughly one-third segments parallel to the back of the car, and then mark them with a pencil.

4. Using the box cutter, cut a semicircular door with straight sides on both sides of the box, from the front one-third section to halfway through the back one-third section.

5. Cut the back two-thirds of the top of the box, leaving the front one-third of the top in place.

6. Fold the back two-thirds portion you just cut, so that one-third of the flap folds up to create the dashboard.

7. With the tip of the box cutter, make a small hole in the middle of the portion of the dashboard that will fold down inside the car. Poke a brad through the middle of a paper plate, and then through the hole you made in the cardboard dashboard.

8. Fold the dashboard down and hot-glue the edges to the sides with the car doors. Hold the cardboard in place until the glue is dry.

(continued)

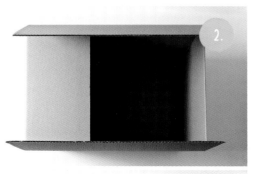

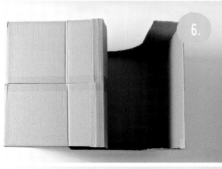

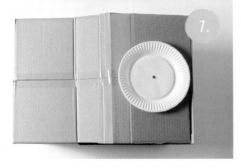

9. Create 4 paper plate wheels. First, place a paper plate on the bottom-right side of the box. Hold the bottom of the plate slightly above the bottom of the box—when the box is on the floor the wheels should not touch the ground. Use the tip of the box cutter to make a small hole through the middle of the plate and through the cardboard. Poke a brad through the hole and open the back of the brad to secure the paper plate wheel. Repeat this process to secure the remaining 3 wheels.

10. Hot-glue the back of the brads to the cardboard, ensuring the wheels will still spin on the outside of the box.

11. Cut the bottoms off the 2 plastic cups with the box cutter or a pair of scissors. With the hot glue gun on low heat, glue the cups to the front of the box to create the car's headlights.

12. If desired, use the paintbrush and nontoxic paint to paint the dashboard and grille to make the car look more realistic. You can also let your child paint the car or draw on the car with crayons. Help baby get in the car and push them around the house, or let them push stuffed animals in the car.

# WIPEABLE CAR PLAY MAT

Create this motorway canvas that will inspire creative, imaginative and active play. Cereal box tunnels, hills and bridges are a fun addition that will help your child learn about how things roll and move. Small babies will enjoy watching you slide cars down the ramps until they are old enough to play independently. It may not seem like much, but kneeling to play encourages core stabilization, and these roads will encourage your child to kneel, play on their stomach or squat—all fantastic, whole-body movements.[11] Clear tape makes this board more durable and creates an easy-to-wipe surface for you or your child to paint buildings, trees, people and whatever else the two of you can imagine.

▲ ▲ ▲

Ruler

Precision crafting knife

Cardboard

Painters' tape

Paintbrush and acrylic paint in black and 2 other colors

2 family-sized cereal boxes

Pencil

Clear packing tape

Scissors

Hot glue gun and glue

Washable kids' paint (optional)

Toy cars

1. With the ruler and precision crafting knife, measure and cut out a piece of cardboard that is approximately 3 x 4 feet (1 x 1.2 m). Use the painters' tape to create the outlines and centerlines of the roads you will paint: Using the ruler for guidance, tape off 6-inch (15-cm)-wide roads with the painters' tape. Use long pieces of tape to easily create straight lines. Overlap the roads to create crossings and T-shaped intersections.

2. Using the precision crafting knife, cut and remove the tape from the road's intersections to create clear roadways. If desired, make centerlines by cutting roughly 1½-inch (4-cm) pieces of painters' tape and adhering them to the middle of the roads to paint over.

3. Paint between the strips of painters' tape and over the centerlines with the black acrylic paint.

4. While the black paint dries, you will create the cereal box tunnels and bridge. Open the cereal boxes and lay them flat. On the blank interior of one of the cereal boxes, measure 2 (6 x 14–inch [15 x 35–cm] or 9 x 16–inch [23 x 40–cm]) sections, marking the sections with the pencil. These sections will be the tunnels. Paint the sections with any color of acrylic paint.

5. To make the bridge, on the blank interior of the other cereal box, measure a 6 x 16–inch (15 x 40–cm) section centered on the spine of the cereal box. The spine of the cereal box will be the elevated portion of the bridge on which cars "drive." Paint the section with any color of acrylic paint.

6. When the black paint is dry, carefully remove the painters' tape. Tape over the entire cardboard sheet with the clear packing tape, overlapping strips of tape that are slightly longer than the cardboard and adhering the ends to the back of the cardboard.

(continued)

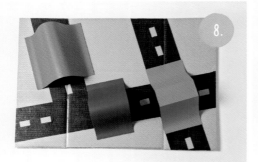

7. When the tunnels' and bridge's paint is dry, cut out the 3 painted pieces with the scissors.

8. Decide where you would like to place your tunnels and bridge, then use the hot glue gun to glue the ends to the taped cardboard.

9. Paint a town or other scene next to the roads with more acrylic paint, or let your toddler paint with washable kids' paint if desired. Acrylic and washable paint will both wipe off with a wet cloth, so you can periodically change out the scene, or your child can paint, wipe and paint again. After the paint is completely dry, let your child explore the roadways with their toy cars.

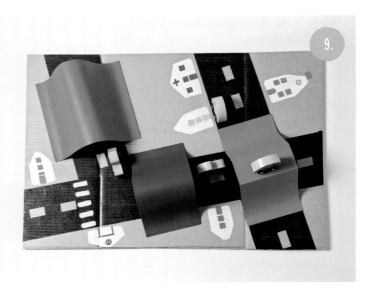

# MAGNETIC FISHING

Create a fine motor fishing game for your child that hones their hand-eye coordination. If your babe isn't ready for the challenge, hang the fish as a mobile, string them onto ribbon to grab or pick up the fish with them. Use this fishing game as a chance to introduce simple terms like "pick up," "let go" and "swim, fish!" Encourage your child to pick up a certain color of fish if they are able, or introduce each fish: "The fish is red."

Permanent marker

Magnetic Fishing Template (page 163)

White computer paper

Scissors

1 (9 x 12" [23 x 30–cm]) sheet of felt in each of the following colors: red, orange, yellow, green, blue and purple (6 sheets total)

6 jumbo paper clips

Hot glue gun and glue

Small Circle Template (page 166)

Clear plastic sheet protector

Button magnet

12" (30-cm) piece of string

2 jumbo craft sticks

1. First, make the fish. With a permanent marker, lightly trace the Magnetic Fishing Template onto a sheet of white paper, then cut out the shapes. Trace them onto each sheet of felt twice, so that you will have 2 fish of each color. Cut the fish out with sharp scissors.

2. Next, attach the paper clips to the fish. This will allow us to "catch" them with the magnetic bait attached to our fishing pole. To do this, place a paper clip on top of 1 fish of each color. The paper clip should extend past the mouth of the fish by approximately ¼ inch (6 mm).

3. Cover a fish and its paper clip with hot glue, being sure to not to apply the glue to the portion of the paper clip extending past the felt.

4. Put the remaining felt fish of the same color on top, lining up the sides. Press firmly so that both sides of the entire fish are adhered to each other and the paper clip is secure between the two layers of felt. Repeat this process for each color of fish.

5. Next, make the magnetic circle we'll use as bait. Trace the Small Circle Template onto a sheet of white paper and cut it out with the scissors. Then, using the scraps from one of the felt sheets, trace the Small Circle twice with the permanent marker. Then trace the Small Circle Template twice onto a clear plastic sheet protector. Cut out the felt and plastic pieces with scissors. When the bait is assembled in the following steps, the magnet will be between the 2 plastic pieces, and the plastic pieces will be between the 2 felt pieces.

6. Place the button magnet on one side of the felt bait, toward the bottom of the shape. Leave enough space around the magnet to glue around all sides of the magnet. Trace the magnet with a permanent marker.

7. Cut the circle out of the felt bait, then trace it onto the same location on the second felt bait and onto 1 piece of the clear plastic bait. Cut the circle out of the second felt bait.

(continued)

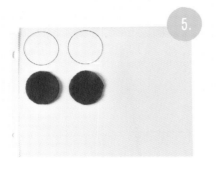

8. Place the magnet over the traced circle on the clear plastic bait. Place one end of the string above the magnet on the same side of the clear plastic bait. With the glue gun on low heat, apply glue over the string's end and the plastic, then adhere the other side of the plastic bait so that the string and magnet are sandwiched between both sides of the bait and the plastic is glued around the entire magnet. Glue should not cover the magnet.

9. With the glue gun on low heat, apply glue to one side of the plastic bait, but not over the magnet. Adhere one of the felt baits so the circular hole lines up with the magnet. Repeat this process on the other side.

10. To create the fishing pole, hot-glue the other end of the string to the end of a jumbo craft stick. Apply hot glue over the string and stick and adhere another jumbo craft stick, so the string is sandwiched between the sticks. When the glue has dried, check that all of the pieces are secure.

11. Set the fish out on the floor or in a tray or bowl and show your child how they can use the fishing pole to "go fishing." If you need to lend a hand, you can hold the pole for your child and let them try to attach the fish, or show your child how they can hold the bait and attach the magnetic bait to the fish.

# POUND-A-BALL

Create a musical pounding toy that can be used to encourage your child to develop fine and gross motor skills. Pushing or pounding the balls into the box takes hand strength and dexterity, and placing the box in various locations can help your child develop prewalking skills. Try putting the box on a slightly elevated surface, like a low table or upside-down storage box. Place the balls on the floor in front of the box, then encourage your child to squat down, grab a ball, stand up and push the ball into the pound-a-ball toy. Squatting and standing are important precursors to cruising and walking. Use this toy on the floor as well, or add a color-matching component by painting different colors around the rims of the holes.

Cardboard shoebox

Paintbrush and acrylic paint

Pencil

3 small balls (such as tennis balls, dryer balls or ball-pit balls)

Precision crafting knife

Pushpin

Ruler

Scissors

String

2 pony beads

3 small bells

1. Paint the shoebox with the acrylic paint, letting the paint dry between coats and using multiple coats to cover the box.

2. With a pencil, lightly trace around one of the balls 3 times on the underside of the shoebox lid. If you find tracing the ball difficult, trace a cup that the ball fits just inside of.

3. The traced holes will need to be the same diameter as the balls in order for your child to push the balls into the shoebox rather than dropping them into the box. Cut the circles out of the box with a precision crafting knife, first cutting them slightly smaller than the diameter you have drawn and testing the fit. Continue to cut the holes slightly larger until the balls can be pushed through.

4. With the pencil, mark the middle of the shoebox's short sides 1¼ inches (3 cm) up from the bottom of the box. Use a pushpin or other sharp object to poke through the mark on the shoebox, then widen the holes so that the string can be threaded through the holes.

5. Using a ruler and scissors, measure and cut a piece of string that is longer than the shoebox—roughly 18 inches (45 cm) long.

6. Thread the string through one hole, and then tie and securely knot a pony bead on the end outside the box.

7. Thread the bells onto the string inside the box. Pull the other end of the string through the opposite hole and pull the string taut. Holding the string taut, tie a pony bead on the end of the string outside of the shoebox.

8. Replace the shoebox's lid and push the bells to line up with the holes. Baby can push the balls through with their hands or with a toy hammer. If you don't have a toy hammer, use a mixing spoon, silicone spatula or upside-down measuring cup.

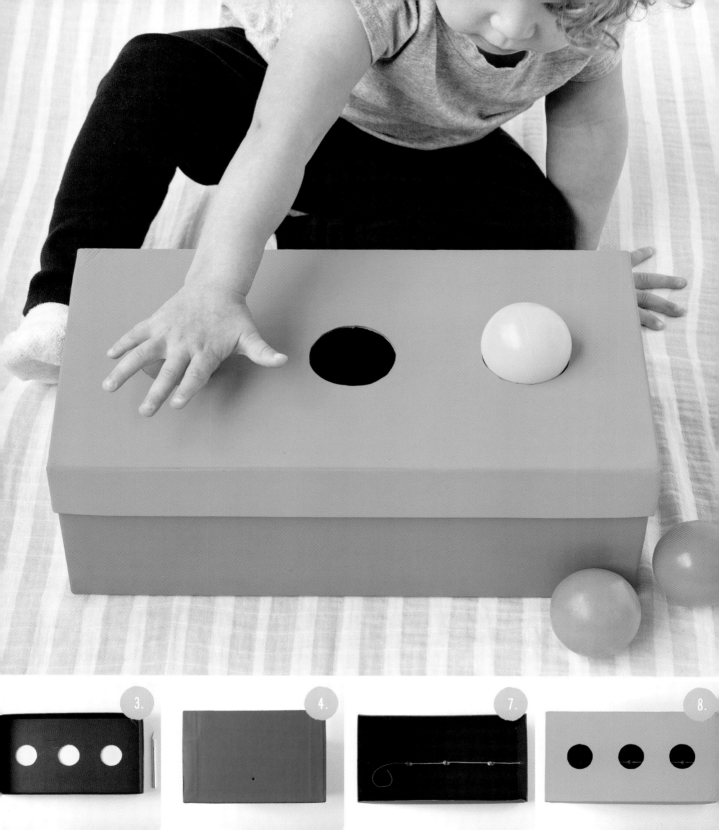

# COLOR CAP MATCH

Create a puzzle for vertical-surface play with recycled plastic lids. Playing on vertical surfaces while seated or standing can help your baby with posture, stability, flexibility and coordination.[12] Strengthening baby's arms and shoulders will lead to better dexterity—all you have to do is lean the puzzle against a wall or piece of furniture. This puzzle is also ideal for use on the floor during tummy time for babies or toddlers—yes, even toddlers benefit from tummy time! Turn this into a game for your toddler by hiding the puzzle pieces and encouraging your child to run to find them, then place them in their proper space.

3 (1½" [4-cm] or larger) plastic lids

Ruler

Precision crafting knife

Cardboard

Pencil

Paintbrush and acrylic paint in 3 colors to match the plastic lids

Hot glue gun and glue

1. Wash the lids and allow them to dry completely prior to using them for this project. Lids from jars of cornstarch, nut butter, pretzels or animal crackers work well for this application.

2. Using the ruler and precision crafting knife, measure and cut 2 (9 x 12–inch [23 x 30–cm]) pieces from the cardboard. The lids will be the puzzle pieces, so if you collected small lids, you can cut out smaller cardboard pieces so that the lids take up roughly 75 percent of a single cardboard piece.

3. Arrange the lids on one of the cardboard pieces, then trace around each lid with a pencil. Cut the circles out of the cardboard. You can discard the cutouts.

4. Lay the piece of cardboard with the open circles on top of the other solid piece of cardboard, and trace inside the circles.

5. Paint the traced circles with the acrylic paint to match the corresponding lid colors. When the paint has dried, apply hot glue to the bottom of the cut cardboard sheet and firmly press the 2 pieces of cardboard together, so that the paint shows through the holes. Allow the glue to dry.

6. Lean the puzzle against a wall to allow your little one to try placing the lids in the correct spots vertically. Alternatively, place the puzzle on a low table or the ground.

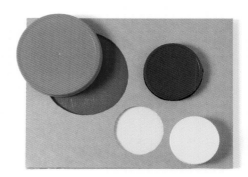

6.

# FELT SHAPE BOARD

As your baby learns to stand, cruise and walk, they may prefer to play standing. A felt board is a great motivator for working on these gross motor skills, as well as fine motor skills required to place the felt objects on the board and remove them. This felt panel can also be used by younger babies during tummy time or even by older children as an inexpensive storyboard. Create any additional felt shapes or objects you like!

Ruler

Pencil

Poster board

Precision crafting knife

Hot glue gun and glue

5 (9 x 12" [23 x 30-cm]) sheets of soft or stiff felt in different colors

White computer paper

Large Circle, Large Triangle, Large Square and Large Hexagon Templates (pages 172–173)

Permanent marker

Scissors

Painters' tape

1. With the ruler and pencil, measure and mark a piece of poster board that is 13½ x 10 inches (34 x 25 cm). Cut out the piece of poster board with the precision crafting knife.

2. Hot-glue a 9 x 12–inch (23 x 30–cm) felt sheet to the middle of the poster board.

3. Trace the Large Circle, Large Triangle, Large Square and Large Hexagon Templates onto the white paper and cut them out. With a permanent marker, trace each cut-out shape onto one of the remaining 4 sheets of felt. Cut out the felt shapes with the scissors.

4. Apply painters' tape to the edges of the poster board around the felt, then tape the felt board to a wall at a height your child can reach.

5. Your little one can stick the shapes to the felt and remove them—no adhesive needed, because the felt sticks to itself when pressed. For babies who are sitting but not standing, tape the board low on the wall and encourage them to lean forward to remove the shapes.

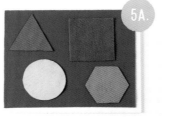

# VIBRANT STRAW ROLLER

If your baby is learning to crawl, a do-it-yourself toy like this straw roller can be just the motivator they need to move. Bright and pleasant-sounding, this bottle can be rolled just out of reach to encourage your little one to wriggle. Use this bottle as a rattle for young babies to watch and listen to. Extend the use of this craft by creating multiple bottle "bowling pins" with different colored straws to knock down with a small ball. This craft is a great way to use rinsed and dried plastic straws from your morning iced coffees!

▲   ▲   ▲

30 plastic or paper straws

Scissors

12- to 20-oz (360- to 600-ml) clear plastic bottle with lid

20 pony beads

Hot glue gun and glue

1. If the straws have been used previously, rinse them and allow them to dry completely.

2. With the scissors, cut each straw into about 5 pieces of roughly equal length.

3. Put the cut straws into the bottle.

4. Add the pony beads to the bottle and secure the bottle's lid. Shake the bottle to distribute the beads.

5. Remove the bottle's lid. Apply hot glue to the inside of the lid, then replace the lid and tighten it on the bottle. Let the glue dry.

6. Use the bottle as a rattle, rolling toy or bowling pin!

5.

# INVESTIGATION AND DISCOVERY

Babies and toddlers are natural investigators! They are eager to learn about, explore and discover their environment. Babies discovering object permanence are fascinated by hiding and revealing objects, and projects like the Family Faces Book (page 43) and Sliding Surprise Box (page 44) are sure to be a hit. Babies and toddlers are also intrigued by challenges, and refining their perception and fine motor skills is both fun and rewarding. Activities like the Lid Stacking Rings (page 51) and Link Drop Box (page 55) provide them with the opportunity to experiment and make adjustments to complete a task. Watching objects move and testing their trajectory is another captivating experience—the Jingle Ball Run (page 47) and Pop Drop (page 59) are superb for little scientists and analysts.

1.

2.

3.

4.

5.

6.

# FAMILY FACES BOOK

Create a family album that is perfect for your baby or toddler to enjoy, with flaps for playing peekaboo. Describe and name each family member or friend when reading this book before bed, or let baby explore the book independently–looking at the faces and lifting the flaps is a great tummy time activity. Babies love human faces and prefer them over other images from infancy.[14] Pairing this love of people with the fine motor challenge and investigative activity of lifting flaps is sure to be a baby and toddler playtime win.

Ruler

Permanent marker

7 (9 x 12" [23 x 30–cm]) sheets of soft felt in different colors

Scissors

Hot glue gun and glue

5 to 10 (4 x 4" [10 x 10–cm] or larger) photographs of friends and family

1 (4 x 4" [10 x 10–cm] or larger) photograph of your child or children

Pom-poms or felt shapes (optional)

1. With the ruler and permanent marker, measure and mark 3 (6 x 12–inch [15 x 30–cm]) pieces of felt. Use the scissors to cut out the felt pieces. Apply hot glue down the middle from top to bottom to one of the pieces to create the book's spine, and place the second sheet of felt on top. Repeat this process for the third felt sheet, applying glue to the middle of the second sheet and placing the third sheet on top.

2. On a work surface, arrange the photos of family and friends and the photo of your child in the order you would like them to appear in the book.

3. Cut out a square piece of felt that measures 4¾ x 4¾ inches (12 x 12 cm) for each photo. Cut the middle out of one of the squares to form a ½-inch (1.3-cm)-thick frame for the cover photo. The remaining squares will be the flaps for the remaining photos.

4. Hot-glue your child's 4 x 4–inch (10 x 10–cm) photo to the middle of the book's cover. Hot-glue 1 (4 x 4–inch [10 x 10–cm]) photo to the middle of each interior page. If you have only 6 photos, hot-glue 1 photo to each right-hand page.

5. Apply a line of hot glue directly above one of the inside photos. Adhere one side of a felt square to form a flap. Repeat this process for each photo. If you want the flaps to open in different directions, apply the glue to different sides of the photos so the flaps will open to the left, to the right or downward.

6. Hot-glue the felt frame over the cover photo. If desired, hot-glue embellishments like pom-poms or felt shapes to the frame. Let your child read, investigate and discover!

# ▲ SLIDING SURPRISE BOX ▲

As your child discovers that objects do not disappear when they are out of sight, they will become fascinated with hiding and finding. This toy is great for strengthening your child's hands, improving coordination and teaching object permanence. Use this two-compartment box with a sliding lid for peekaboo with a ball, or use it as a treasure box–put safe, assorted household objects or toys in the box for your child to discover. Young babies may need some help with sliding the top. Show them how they can drop a ball in the hole, slide the lid together and then let them discover the ball in the compartment!

Precision crafting knife

Cardboard box that is 7" (18 cm) wide or less and at least 5" (13 cm) deep

Paintbrush and acrylic paint (optional)

Ruler

Cardboard

Pencil

Ball (such as a ball-pit ball or tennis ball)

Hot glue gun and glue

Masking tape

1. With the precision crafting knife, cut the top flaps off of the cardboard box and save the flaps. If desired, paint the outside of the box with acrylic paint.

2. To form the lid, use the ruler and precision crafting knife to measure and cut 2 pieces of cardboard to one-half the length of the inside of the box by the inside width of the box. For example, if the box measures 12 inches (30 cm) long by 6 inches (15 cm) wide on the inside, cut 2 pieces of cardboard that measure 6 x 6 inches (15 x 15 cm).

3. With a pencil, trace a ball onto one of the cardboard pieces. Alternatively, trace a circular cup slightly larger than the ball. Cut out the traced circle, then trace the circle onto the other cardboard piece, and then cut out that circle as well. When the 2 cardboard pieces are stacked together, the holes should align. Hot-glue the pieces together to form the lid. Tape the sliding edges of the lid with masking tape.

4. To form the middle partition, cut a long sheet of cardboard 1 inch (2.5 cm) shorter than the inside height of the box. Cut a sliver off the cardboard sheet that is the thickness of the cardboard lid; for example, ¼ inch (6 mm) if the cardboard lid is ¼ inch (6 mm) thick.

5. Cut the long cardboard sheet into 2 pieces the same width as the inside of the box. For example, if your box is 6 inches (15 cm) wide on the inside, cut 2 (6-inch [15-cm])-wide pieces of cardboard. Hot glue the 2 pieces together to form the interior partition.

6. Apply hot glue to the sides and bottom of the partition, then carefully adhere it to the inside of the box in the middle.

7. Cut the reserved long box flaps into 8 (½-inch [1.3-cm]-wide) strips. Hot-glue the strips together in pairs, ensuring they are lined up evenly. Hot-glue one pair on each long side of the box, on top of the partition. The lid should lay flat on top of the strips.

8. With the lid in place, hot-glue the remaining pairs of strips to the box's sides above the lid. The strips need to be against the lid, but check to make sure that the lid can move by sliding it back and forth. Then hold the strips in place while the glue dries. Your child can drop a ball in the hole, then slide the lid to reveal it.

Babies and toddlers who love dropping items from their high chairs or throwing toys are learning how things move! Support this trajectory schema–or repeated behavioral pattern that allows your child to explore motion–with this fun and easy ball-run box. Your child will also learn cause and effect as they notice that a ball running through the end hole causes the bell to ring. Add a creative element to this craft by letting your child decorate the outside of the ball-run box with paint, crayons or markers.

Ruler

Box cutter

Cardboard box that measures at least 16 x 20" (40 x 50 cm)

Hot glue gun and glue

Paintbrush and acrylic paint in 4 colors

4 cardboard paper towel tubes

Scissors

Masking tape

Ball-pit ball or other lightweight ball

Pencil

4" (10 cm) ribbon

Lighter

Small bell

1. With the ruler and box cutter, measure and cut the cardboard box down to a depth of 6 inches (15 cm).

2. Hot-glue the box's bottom flaps to each other if they are only taped together.

3. Paint a little more than half of 3 of the paper towel tubes, so that when you eventually cut the tubes in half lengthwise, you will have one painted half that will become a ramp. Paint the entire surface of the remaining paper towel tube.

4. When the paint is dry, cut all 4 of the paper towel tubes in half lengthwise with scissors. Keep the painted portions of the 3 tubes and discard the unpainted portions. Keep both halves of the fully painted tube.

5. To create the ramps, use the masking tape to secure the halves of the paper towel tubes to the box in the pattern shown. Tape the 2 halves painted the same color together to create the bottom ramp.

6. Test whether a ball rolls correctly, and move the ramps as needed. Mark the locations of the ramps with a pencil. The ball will be easier to keep on the track if the box is tilted at an angle; for example, against a couch.

7. To create the start of the ball run, trace the ball or the rim of a circular cup that the can hold the ball at the top-right corner of the box. Create a hole for the ball to roll through at the end of the ball run by drawing a rectangle or arch slightly wider than the ball at the bottom-right side of the box, aligned with the bottom of the ramp.

8. Cut the circle and arch out with the box cutter.

9. Seal the ends of the ribbon by running them over the lighter's flame. Tie a small bell onto one end of the ribbon and hot-glue it to the box so the bell hangs in the arch.

10. Remove the tape from the ramps and hot-glue the 2 matching tubes together to form the bottom ramp. Hot-glue the remaining ramps in place.

11. Roll the ball down the ramps and hear the bell jingle. If the ball won't stay on course, lean the box back slightly against a couch or wall.

# EGG CARTON COLOR SORT

Present objects in a new way and give your child an opportunity to begin recognizing colors. Blocks, balls, links, lids and other items are all more exciting in this variation on a Montessori treasure basket than on their own. Try adding items that have different textures, shapes and weights for your child to discover. Let your toddler try to place the correct colored objects in the holes—or place them for your little one, then see if they realize the items match. Use this as a receptacle for sorting colorful beads, pom-poms or buttons for crafts when your toddler is older!

1. Ensure that the paper egg carton has not held any broken eggs and that the eggs it has contained have been only pasteurized, store-bought eggs.

2. Paint the inside of the egg compartments with acrylic paint, ensuring there are 2 compartments of each color. Or paint the compartments in any combination you prefer. Allow the paint to fully dry between coats—you may need 2 or 3 coats of paint to cover the compartments.

3. When the paint is dry, put an assortment of colorful, safe objects in the carton for your baby. For a toddler, set the items out adjacent to the carton and encourage them to sort the items into the carton.

▲ ▲ ▲

Paper egg carton

Paintbrush and acrylic paint in rainbow colors

Assorted colorful small items and toys

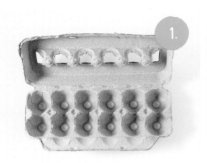 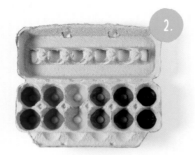 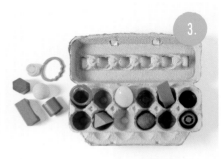

# ▲ LID STACKING RINGS ▲

Stacking, unstacking and organizing objects by size are all important coordination and developmental milestones for your child. These complex tasks take time to master, and starting your baby out with a simple stacking toy is a great way to encourage them to learn and explore. They will begin by removing rings from the toy, then they may move on to stacking two to three rings, ultimately learning to stack the rings on the center pole. Toddlers will learn how to sort the rings according to size through trial and error, then stack them in order on the pole. With just recycled lids and hot glue, you can make a stacking toy that develops your child's mind and body.

Plastic lids (see step 1)

Alcohol swab

Hot glue gun and glue

Standard-sized hot glue stick or 1 (6" [15-cm]-long) wooden dowel (see step 3)

Drill

½" (1.3-cm) drill bit

Serrated knife

1. Collect colorful, thick plastic lids from various food containers, like those found on containers of animal crackers, nut butters, peanuts, pretzels and spices. Look for the code #5 PP on the plastic—these lids will hold up well to drilling and be sturdy enough for stacking. The lids should all be 1½ inches (4 cm) in diameter or larger to avoid choking hazards. You can use as few as 3 lids, or as many as can fit on the standard-sized hot glue stick, which will act as the center pole for the stacker. You will also need 1 small lid, like one from a sports drink bottle, to stabilize the center pole.

2. Remove any text, like date stamps, from the lids with an alcohol swab.

3. Apply hot glue to the inside of the small sports drink lid. Place the standard-sized hot glue stick into the hot glue and hold it upright until the glue dries. If preferred, you can follow the same directions with a wooden dowel instead of a hot glue stick. If you use a dowel, choose the size of your drill bit accordingly.

4. Using a drill fitted with a ½-inch (1.3-cm) drill bit, carefully drill a hole in the center of each of the remaining lids—a drill bit made for plastic is preferable, but not essential. Place each lid with its bottom facing downward on a slip-resistant surface that will not be damaged by the drill—like plywood—then slowly drill in the middle of the lid.

5. If any plastic remains attached to the holes, cut it off with a serrated knife.

6. Feed the hot glue stick attached to the sports drink lid through the hole in the largest lid, which will act as a base. Pull the small lid back out far enough to apply hot glue to the inside of the base where the rim of the small lid will be adhered. Turn the base upright, with the hot glue stick pointing upward, and pull the hot glue stick firmly while the hot glue dries and sets to secure the small lid to the large base lid.

7. Stack the remaining lids in order on the glue stick pole. With a serrated knife, cut the top of the glue stick level with the top lid. Let your child try to remove the lids from the pole and restack them.

# ▲ PAJAMA PULL ▲

This fine motor toy encourages investigation and gives new life to stained bodysuits! Babies and toddlers love to pull tissues and wipes from boxes; these tabs are less messy to pull and can easily be restuffed. Your baby will begin pulling with a palmar grasp, using their whole hand and palm to pull. With practice, at around nine months old, your baby will pull with a more refined pincer grasp, using their thumb and forefinger. Give them the opportunity to strengthen and improve their grasp while exploring! Toddlers can pull the pajama arms and attempt to stuff the arms back into the pockets as well.

▲  ▲  ▲

Ruler

Scissors

2 to 3 long-sleeved bodysuits or 3 (2 x 6" [5 x 15–cm]) strips of felt

Pencil

9 x 12" (23 x 30–cm) sheet of soft felt

Cardboard

Precision crafting knife

Permanent marker

Hot glue gun and glue

1. With the ruler and scissors, measure and cut 6 inches (15 cm) off the long-sleeved arms of the bodysuits. If you are using strips of felt, skip this step and proceed to step 2.

2. Using a pencil, trace the felt sheet onto the cardboard. Use the precision crafting knife to cut the cardboard the same size as the felt.

3. With a permanent marker, create 3 evenly spaced lines that are the width of the bodysuit arms, about 2 inches (5 cm) wide, on the felt sheet.

4. Using scissors, cut the drawn lines to form slits. Lay the felt over the cardboard and trace the slits onto the cardboard with a pencil.

5. Hot-glue the cut ends of the bodysuit arms onto the cardboard 1 inch (2.5 cm) below the lines. First, hot-glue the layer of fabric closest to the cardboard, then apply hot glue between the layers of fabric to seal the sleeves and secure them.

6. Apply hot glue to the cardboard in the following locations: above the lines drawn by tracing the felt slits, next to the lines and at the bottom of the cardboard. Leave an empty rectangular area below each glued sleeve to form the felt pockets, into which you will stuff the sleeves. Place the felt on top of the glue to adhere it to the cardboard.

7. Loosen and stretch the felt pockets, then stuff the sleeves inside them. Young babies can pull the arms, and toddlers can try to pull and re-stuff the arms independently.

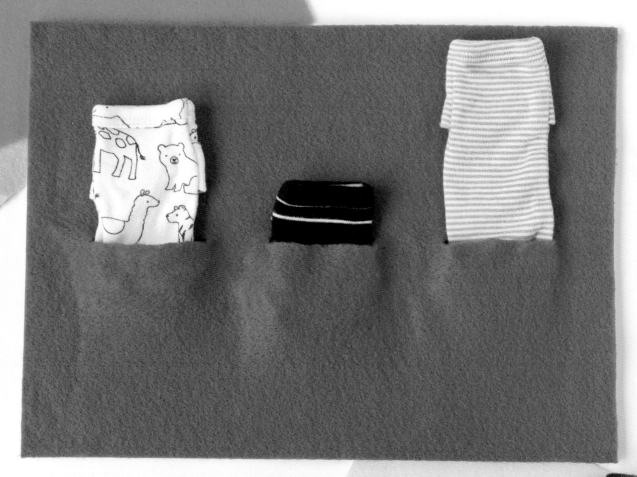

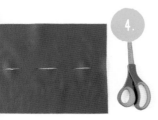
4.

5.

6.

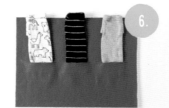

7.

# LINK DROP BOX

Repurpose baby wipe lids and create a fun activity. Babies and toddlers master new skills through trial and error, learning how to complete a task each time they make a mistake or succeed. Lifting a lid, turning a link and dropping the link into a hole may seem simple, but going through this process and continuously asking themselves questions like "What will happen if I do this?" and "Will it fit this way?" will help your child create an accurate mental model. Add stickers or paint the top of the lids different colors if you want to make this a color-matching activity for your toddler! If you don't have toy links, use any toy that fits through the holes of wipe lids.

Paintbrush and acrylic paint (optional)

Small cardboard box or shoebox

Hot glue gun and glue

4 standard-sized or 2 large baby wipe lids

Pencil

Precision crafting knife or box cutter

Circular cup about 4" (10 cm) in diameter

Toy links or similar items

Stickers (optional)

1. If desired, paint the outside of the cardboard box with acrylic paint. Allow the paint to fully dry.

2. To glue the box shut, apply hot glue to the underside of one of the box's long outer flaps and adhere it to the inner flaps. Repeat this step for the other outer flap.

3. Lay the baby wipe lids on top of the box and trace the lids' holes with a pencil.

4. Remove the lids and cut the holes out of the box with a precision crafting knife.

5. On one side of the box, trace the circular cup. Cut out the circle to make a hole big enough for an adult hand. If desired, keep the circle cutout to close the hole.

6. Apply hot glue around the top holes, one at a time, and adhere a baby wipe lid to each hole.

7. When the glue has dried, your child can drop links or other items through the holes. If desired, apply stickers to the baby wipe lids or paint their tops different colors if you would like to make this a color-sorting activity.

# ▲ SMILEY CARDS AND WALLET ▲

Babies and toddlers love to sift through purses and wallets. Distract your child from going through your wallet by providing them with their own! Encourage them to look in the pockets of this homemade wallet and to slide the cards in and remove them. Make small cards out of pictures of family and friends to hide and find—babies learn from and enjoy looking at faces. Around nine months old, babies may even begin to recognize familiar faces in a photograph. Toddlers will have fun recalling the name of each person and imagining they are a grown-up using their cards to buy things.

▲   ▲   ▲

Ruler

Scissors

6 or more photographs of family and friends

Clear packing tape or laminating pouches

Permanent marker

1 (9 x 12" [23 x 30-cm]) sheet of stiff felt, plus additional sheets in multiple colors if desired

Clothes iron

Hot glue gun and glue

1. With the ruler and scissors, measure and cut the photographs down to wallet size: 3 x 2 inches (8 x 5 cm). Pictures with large, smiling faces are a great option.

2. Lay a piece of packing tape that is slightly larger than the picture sticky side up, then overlap it with another piece of tape by about ¼ inch (6 mm). Place a picture face side down on the tape. To make double-sided cards, place another picture face side up on top of the first picture.

3. Place a piece of packing tape over the photos, then overlap it with another piece of tape by about ¼ inch (6 mm). The photograph should be covered by tape on both sides. Repeat this process for all of the photographs.

4. Trim each photograph, leaving a ⅛- to ¼-inch (3- to 6-mm) border of tape and rounding the corners.

5. To make the wallet, use the ruler and permanent marker to measure and mark a 9 x 7–inch (23 x 18–cm) section of felt and cut it out. Cut 2 (4 x 1¾–inch [10 x 4–cm]) pieces and 2 (4 x 2¾–inch [10 x 7–cm]) pieces from the same felt sheet or the different colored sheets (if using).

6. Bring the clothes iron to medium heat. Fold the 9 x 7–inch (23 x 18–cm) felt sheet in half lengthwise, then iron it until a crease forms—be careful not to iron the felt so long that it begins to melt. Fold it in half lengthwise again and then iron the felt a second time until a crease forms. This process will create the middle crease of the wallet.

7. Unfold the felt. Apply a thin line of hot glue to both of the short ends of the felt. Then fold the felt lengthwise how it was ironed so that it forms one long pocket that is folded in the middle, with the edges glued. This process forms the billfold pocket. To form the card pockets, apply a thin line of hot glue to the bottom and sides of the 4 x 1¾–inch (10 x 4–cm) felt pieces, then adhere them to the 4 x 2¾–inch (10 x 7–cm) pieces, aligning the long sides.

8. Apply a thin line of hot glue to the bottom and sides of the card pockets, then adhere them to the billfold, aligning the left and right sides with the wallet. When the glue has dried, place the cards in your child's new wallet. Now it is full of friendly faces for some fine motor fun!

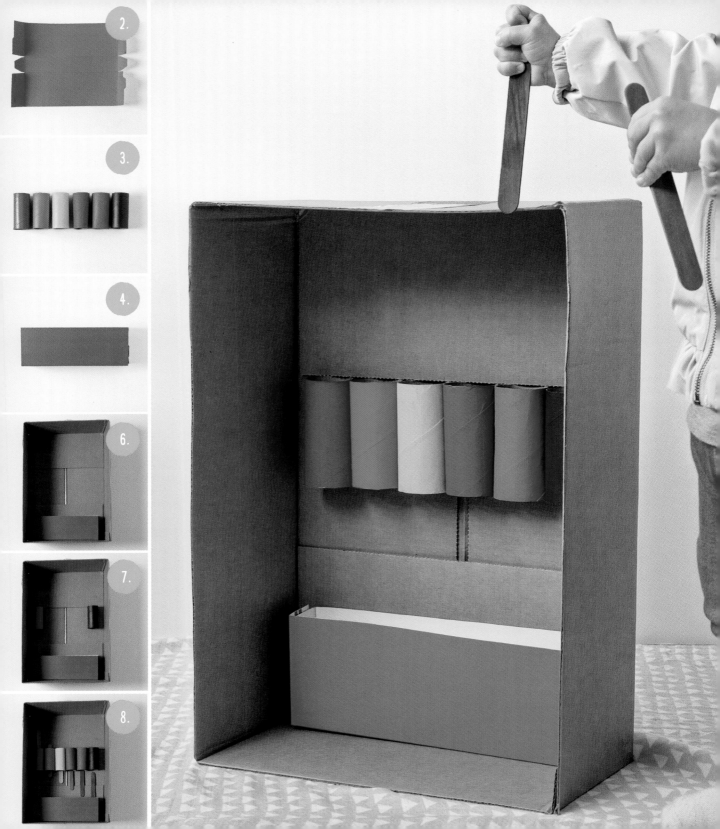

# POP DROP

Your baby or toddler can sort ice pop sticks by color or drop different materials like straws, O-shaped cereal or ping-pong balls through these vibrant tubes. Your child will explore motion, learn about cause and effect and work on fine motor skills–all while having fun. Expand on this activity with an older toddler by putting letter stickers on the tubes and encouraging your child to sort foam letters. Use this as a way to make simple addition tangible: If your toddler puts one stick through one tube and one through another, how many sticks will end up in the box?

▲ ▲ ▲

Standard-sized cereal box

Ruler

Pencil

Precision crafting knife

Paintbrush and acrylic paint in rainbow colors

6 toilet paper tubes

Hot glue gun and glue

Box cutter

Cardboard box measuring at least 12 x 16" (30 x 40 cm)

Jumbo ice pop sticks, clothespins or balls in rainbow colors

1. To form a receptacle for the sticks to drop into, disassemble the cereal box and use the ruler and pencil to measure and mark the sides, so that the box will measure 4 inches (10 cm) tall when it is reassembled. Cut the cereal box at the marked locations with the precision crafting knife.

2. Paint the blank inside of the cereal box with acrylic paint.

3. While the paint on the cereal box dries, paint the toilet paper tubes with acrylic paint. You can paint each toilet paper roll a different color of the rainbow to encourage your child to sort by color.

4. When the cereal box is dry, reassemble it inside out so that the painted side faces outward. Hot-glue the sides and bottom of the cereal box shut.

5. Using the ruler and box cutter, measure and cut the cardboard box so that it measures 5 or 6 inches (13 or 15 cm) deep. The interior bottom of the cardboard box will be the vertical surface to which you glue the toilet paper tubes and cereal box.

6. Hot-glue the broad side of the cereal box to the interior bottom of the cardboard box.

7. The painted toilet paper tubes will be glued to the interior bottom of the cardboard box in a row above the cereal box. Begin by hot-gluing the 2 outer toilet paper tubes in the row to what will be the vertical middle of the box, directly above the cereal box. Space out the remaining toilet paper rolls and hot-glue them between the first and last rolls.

8. Baby can put jumbo ice pop sticks, clothespins or balls through the tubes and watch them drop.

# SHADOW PROJECTOR TUBES

Cast shadows for fun or learning with these simple projector tubes. Draw letters, numbers, shapes or animals to spark your child's curiosity– light and shadow make the mundane magical for all ages. Draw animals, then create a shadow theater for storytelling. Make a challenge for your older toddler by drawing a shape on paper and taping it to the wall. Draw the same shape on the tube, then have your child shine a light and try to line up the shapes.

Permanent marker

1 paper towel tube, plus more if desired

Clear plastic take-out or fruit container lid

Precision crafting knife

Paintbrush and acrylic paint (optional)

Cloth

Hot glue gun and glue

Black dry-erase marker

1. With a permanent marker, trace the end of a paper towel tube onto a clear plastic take-out lid. If you are using more than 1 paper towel tube, draw 1 circle for each projector tube you plan to make.

2. Cut the circles out with a precision crafting knife.

3. If desired, paint the paper towel tube with acrylic paint and allow the paint to fully dry.

4. Wipe any dirt or fingerprints off the clear plastic circle with a cloth. Apply a thin line of hot glue around the rim of the circle, then adhere it to the end of the paper towel roll. Repeat this process for each additional projector tube, if needed.

5. Draw a shape, animal, letter or number on the clear circle with a dry-erase marker.

6. Shine a light through the opposite end of the tube in a dark room to project the image onto a wall. Wipe the dry-erase marker off the circle with a dry cloth, then draw another image. Let your child try holding the tube to project the image.

# HIDE-AND-FIND POUCHES

Babies and toddlers are fascinated by trinkets and need a place to keep their special objects! They love hiding and finding, and these pouches are a perfect tool for enveloping and hiding small toys or nature items. Closing and reopening these pouches and playing hide-and-seek with the treasures they contain will be a favorite game for on-the-go fun. Use these pouches as sustainable, reusable gift wrap as well! Opening and closing the pouches is a great fine motor challenge, and they can be used to teach your child how to tie and untie bows.

Permanent marker

9" (23-cm) round plate

3 (9 x 12" [23 x 30-cm]) sheets of soft felt in different colors

Scissors

Ruler

2 yards (2 m) string

Masking tape

1. With a permanent marker, trace the plate onto a felt sheet. Repeat this step with the other 2 sheets of felt. Cut the circles out with the scissors.

2. Use the permanent marker to make 16 dots around the felt circle, using the ruler to ensure the dots are located ¾ inch (2 cm) inside the perimeter of the felt. To space the dots fairly evenly, draw 2 dots opposite each other, 1 on the left in the 9 o'clock position and 1 on the right in the 3 o'clock position. Then draw 2 more dots to form a cross, 1 on the top in the 12 o'clock position and 1 at the bottom in the 6 o'clock position. Draw 3 dots, roughly evenly spaced, in between each pair of dots.

3. With sharp scissors, cut a small slit that is no more than ⅛ inch (3 mm) wide in the felt at each dot.

4. Cut 1 (24-inch [63-cm]) length of string for each pouch (3 total). Wrap one end of the string with masking tape to make threading the string easier.

5. Thread the string in and out of the slits in the felt. The ends should come out of 2 adjacent holes, with 2 inches (5 cm) of excess string remaining. Remove the tape and triple-knot the string's ends.

6. Fill the pouches with trinkets that are safe for your child or a small ball to hide and find, then pull the strings to close the pouches. Tie a bow to secure them.

# DEXTERITY- AND COORDINATION-BUILDING PLAY

Activities that encourage the development of fine motor skills are an important part of play for babies and toddlers. Grasping, pinching, pulling, twisting, placing and drawing promote manual dexterity, improve coordination and strengthen your baby's muscles.[10] With these toys and activities, like the Smiling Face Puzzle (page 75), Counting Bead Slide (page 79) and Bat-and-Play Ribbon Octopus (page 80), your baby can develop fine motor skills, learn and have fun!

Create a travel toy ideal for supervised car or airplane rides or for simply entertaining your child at home. Babies who are not ready to match colors or shapes will enjoy pulling the shapes off of the board. Older babies and toddlers can attempt to attach the shapes to the fasteners and eventually to the corresponding shape and color. They will also benefit from the challenge of putting the pieces in the pocket and removing them. Add to this craft in the future by punching holes in the sides, adding additional pages and attaching the pages with yarn to create a busy book.

Ruler

Pencil

Cardboard

Precision crafting knife

Paintbrush and acrylic paint in white or light gray (optional)

Small Heart, Small Circle, Small Diamond, Small Triangle and Small Square Templates (page 166)

White computer paper

Scissors

Permanent markers in red, orange, yellow, green and blue

6 (5 x 5" [13 x 13-cm]) sheets of soft felt in red, orange, yellow, green, blue and purple

Hot glue gun and glue

Small hook-and-loop fastener dots or strips (such as VELCRO® Brand fasteners)

1. Using the ruler and pencil, measure and mark a 9 x 9–inch (23 x 23–cm) square on the cardboard. Cut out the square with the precision crafting knife. If desired, paint the cardboard with the acrylic paint.

2. Trace the Small Heart Template onto a sheet of white paper and cut it out with scissors. With a permanent marker, trace the heart cutout twice onto the red felt, then cut out the felt hearts. Repeat this process for each shape on the orange, yellow, green and blue felt. Cut out a 3-inch (8-cm) square pocket from the purple felt.

3. Hot-glue the pairs of shapes together with a generous amount of glue. The glue will help stiffen the shapes. When the glue has dried, use scissors to cut off any glue that overflowed out of the shapes.

4. With permanent markers in corresponding colors, trace the small templates onto the dry, painted cardboard, leaving room for the square pocket.

5. Apply hot glue to the edges of the bottom and sides of the purple square pocket, and adhere it to the cardboard. Apply hot glue to the back of the hook sides of the hook-and-loop fastener dots, or cut strips of the hook-and-loops fasteners to fit within the shape outlines. Adhere them in the center of the shape outlines on the cardboard.

6. When the glue dries, place the felt shapes on the hook fasteners—they will act as the loop sides and adhere even if they are placed off-center. Your child can remove the shapes, place them in the pocket and reattach them.

# ▲ RIBBON SHAPES PUZZLE ▲

Before your child begins matching shapes and colors, they can begin to recognize them with the aid of this DIY puzzle. The ribbon handles are ideal for babies who are currently grabbing things between their fingers and palm. As your child's grasp progresses, they can grab the ribbons between their thumb and forefinger. Encourage language development by repeating "grab" when your baby grabs the ribbons, and "pull" when they pull each piece. For toddlers, present the challenge of matching the pieces and placing them correctly in each hole.

Ruler

Precision crafting knife

Cardboard

Pencil

Large Square, Large Circle and Large Triangle Templates (pages 172–173)

White computer paper

Scissors

Paintbrush and acrylic paint in 3 colors

3 (8" [20-cm]-long) pieces of ribbon in 3 colors

Lighter

Hot glue gun and glue

1. With the ruler and precision crafting knife, measure and cut out 2 (8 x 15–inch [20 x 38–cm]) sheets of cardboard. With a pencil, trace the Large Square, Large Circle and Large Triangle Templates onto sheets of white paper. Cut the shapes out of the paper with scissors, then trace these cutouts onto one of the cardboard sheets, being sure to space them evenly.

2. Cut out the shapes carefully with a precision crafting knife to create the puzzle pieces. Test the fit of the puzzle pieces into the holes, and cut the holes slightly larger to make the puzzle less challenging, so that the pieces fit in any correct orientation.

3. Place the cut cardboard over the intact cardboard sheet, and trace the holes lightly. Paint the individual puzzle pieces, and then paint inside the traced shapes on the intact cardboard—don't worry about painting outside the lines, as this area will be covered.

4. Run the ends of the ribbons quickly over the flame of a lighter to seal them.

5. When the paint has dried, apply a thin line of hot glue to the backs of the puzzle pieces, then adhere the ribbons. Test the fit of the puzzle pieces in the holes again, and cut the holes slightly larger if necessary.

6. Apply hot glue around the painted portions of the bottom intact cardboard piece, then adhere the top cardboard piece with the cutouts, so that the paint shows through the puzzle piece holes.

7. Place the puzzle pieces in the holes, so your baby or toddler can use their palm or fingers to remove the pieces using the ribbon.

# JUMBO RAINBOW CRAYONS

Give new life to old, broken crayons, and create fun crayon shapes that are large and easy for your child to hold without breaking or fitting in their mouth. Experiment with various shapes using silicone molds, or use standard or mini muffin tins. These beautiful crayons also make an inexpensive party favor or gift! Create multicolor crayons by combining different colors in each mold. Make exciting, terrazzo-like rainbow crayons of any hue, and use them to draw unique pictures.

Crayons in any colors (see step 1)

Standard-sized muffin tin, mini muffin tin or silicone baking mold

1. Gather broken crayons—you will need about 6 standard crayons to fill a standard-sized muffin cup. Keep in mind that regardless of the type of mold you choose, you will need enough broken crayons to fill the mold halfway.

2. Place an oven rack in the middle of the oven. Preheat the oven to 300°F (150°C).

3. Remove the paper wrappers from the crayons and discard them.

4. Break the crayons into ½-inch (1.3-cm) segments or smaller and fill the muffin cups or silicone baking molds half full. Try putting like colors together, or make any rainbow combination. You can make as few as 1 jumbo crayon, or as many as your muffin tin or baking mold allows.

5. Place the muffin tin on the oven's middle rack and let the crayons melt for 10 to 15 minutes.

6. When the wax has completely melted, remove the muffin tin and set it on a heatproof surface to cool at room temperature for at least 4 hours.

7. When the wax has completely hardened and cooled, turn the muffin tin over and hit the bottom of the muffin cups to loosen the jumbo crayons. The crayons should fall out easily. If they do not, place the muffin tin in the refrigerator for 5 minutes, then try again. Let your child explore drawing with their colorful crayons!

# ▲ SPINNING COLOR WHEEL ▲

This colorful toy will delight your baby or toddler, and it can improve your child's dexterity and problem-solving skills. You can spin the color wheel for young babies to observe, and older babies and toddlers can spin it independently. Watch your toddler's mental wheels turn as they attempt to rotate and match the colors. This activity can help introduce geometry, math and color theory—a precursor to future STEAM (Science, Technology, Engineering, Arts and Math) challenges.

▲  ▲  ▲

Ruler

Pencil

Cardboard

Precision crafting knife

Large Circle Template (page 173)

White computer paper

Scissors

Paintbrush and acrylic paint in rainbow colors

Brad paper fastener

Hot glue gun and glue

1. Using the ruler and pencil, measure and mark a 6 x 6–inch (15 x 15–cm) square on the cardboard. Cut out the square with the precision crafting knife. Trace the Large Circle Template onto a sheet of white paper and cut it out with scissors. Then trace the cutout onto another piece of cardboard and cut it out.

2. Measure 1¼ inches (3 cm) from the top and bottom of the square and mark 4 points on the edges, with 2 marks on the left edge and 2 marks on the right edge. Connect the points with the ruler and pencil to create diagonal lines.

3. Use the ruler and pencil to measure and mark 3 inches (8 cm) inward from the middle of the top edge and the middle of the bottom edge of the cardboard. Draw a vertical line with a pencil to connect these marks through the middle of the diagonal lines. There will now be 6 sections drawn on the cardboard.

4. Place the circle in the center of the square, and trace around the circle with a pencil. Trace the lines on the square onto the circle.

5. Paint each section of the square and circle a different color, in the order of the rainbow. Allow the paint to dry, then apply additional coats as necessary.

6. Cut a small slit in the center of the square and circle with a precision crafting knife, then insert a brad paper fastener through the circle and square. Open the back of the brad and rotate the circle until it moves freely.

7. Hot-glue the back of the brad and allow the glue to dry, so the fastener cannot be removed. Alternatively, cut another 6 x 6–inch (15 x 15–cm) cardboard square and hot-glue it to the back to cover the brad. Once the glue dries, your child can spin the wheel and match the colors!

# ▲ SMILING FACE PUZZLE ▲

This puzzle will help develop your baby's pincer grasp and delight them at the same time! Your child will be fascinated by hiding and finding the face behind the puzzle piece on their own or with a little help from you. Use the puzzle as a tummy time activity for an infant by removing the puzzle piece and propping the frame in front of baby. For babies and toddlers nine months old and older, place the puzzle on the ground and let your child try to remove and then replace the puzzle piece. The picture of a parent, grandparent or other familiar face will encourage baby to keep trying to master this puzzle.

Ruler

Precision crafting knife

Cardboard

Circular cup measuring 3" (8 cm) in diameter

Pencil

Paintbrush and acrylic paint (optional)

3" (8-cm) or larger square photograph of a family member

Hot glue gun and glue

Pony bead or pom-pom

1. Using the ruler and precision crafting knife, measure and cut out 2 (6-inch [15-cm]) square pieces of cardboard.

2. Create the frame. In the center of one of the cardboard pieces, trace around the circular cup with a pencil.

3. To create the puzzle piece, cut the traced circle out of the cardboard frame using a precision crafting knife. Trim the circular puzzle piece so it fits easily into the hole you created without needing to be perfectly aligned.

4. If desired, paint one side of the cardboard frame and the circular puzzle piece with a layer of acrylic paint. Apply an additional coat of paint when the first coat has dried.

5. Using the precision crafting knife, cut the photograph so it fits onto the cardboard base with the image centered in the circular hole. Hot-glue the back of the photo to the cardboard base, so the image will be centered in the circular opening of the frame.

6. Hot-glue the unpainted side of the cardboard frame to the mounted photo. The two cardboard squares should align.

7. Hot-glue a pony bead or pom-pom to the middle of the painted cardboard circle to create the puzzle piece. Present the puzzle to your baby once the glue is fully dried, and watch them uncover the hidden face!

# ▲ RING BOX PULL ▲

Grabbing and pulling the rings on this toy take refined movement and coordination, as well as big-muscle force! This three-dimensional toy can also encourage spatial and directional awareness as you talk to your child about pulling the links around, under, over, left or right. Make a game for your toddler by naming a color and seeing if they can pull that link. Or challenge them to find a ring on the top or side. If it is too difficult for your baby to hold the box and pull, you can hold the box and reset the ribbons for them. Add another fun element by hiding little toys in the box for your toddler to feel and grab through the hole.

▲  ▲  ▲

Small cardboard box

Precision crafting knife

Clear packing tape

White butcher paper or wrapping paper

Pencil

Circular cup to trace

Pushpin or other sharp object

Ballpoint pen

6 (18" [45-cm]-long) pieces of ribbon or yarn in rainbow colors

Lighter

6 toy links, teething rings or large scrunchies in rainbow colors

1. Using the precision crafting knife, cut the smaller top interior flaps from the cardboard box. Tape the larger top flaps shut with the clear packing tape.

2. Wrap the box like a present with the butcher paper.

3. Using a pencil, trace a circular cup onto the middle of one side of the box. Cut the circle out with the precision crafting knife—the hole should be large enough for an adult hand.

4. With a pushpin, poke 3 holes in the top and 3 holes in the long side of the box, opposite the large cutout hole. Enlarge the holes with a ballpoint pen.

5. Run the ends of the ribbon quickly over the flame of a lighter to seal them. If you are using yarn, skip this step.

6. Tie each ribbon to a toy link of the same color.

7. Feed the opposite ends of the ribbons through the small holes, then insert your hand into the large hole to pull each ribbon through the large hole. Tie a double knot at the end of each ribbon, then push the ribbons into the box. Your child can pull the rings, then you can reset them by pulling the ribbons in the box.

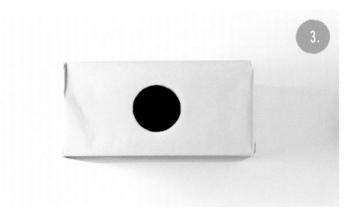

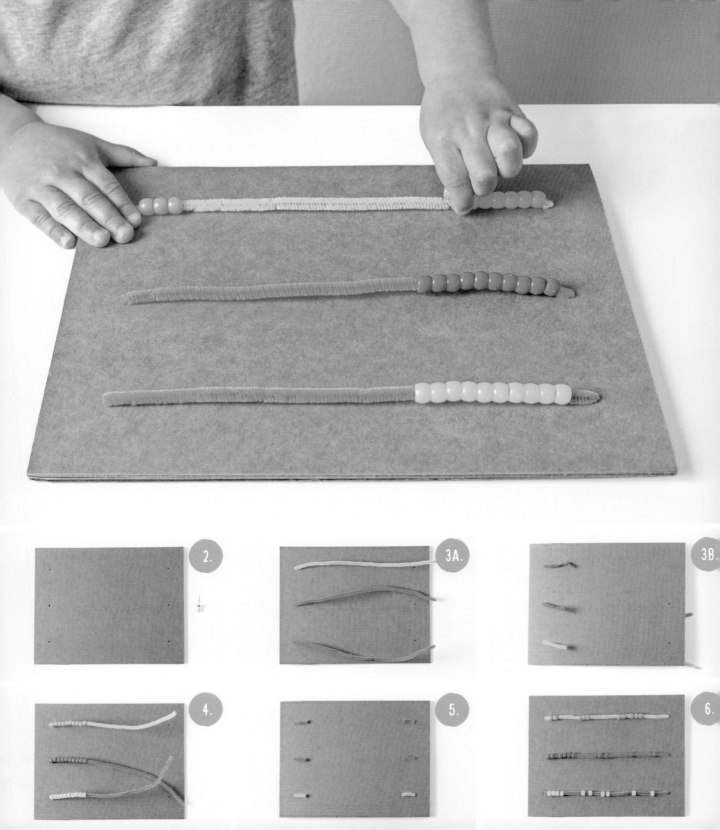

# ▲ COUNTING BEAD SLIDE ▲

This activity helps develop a refined pincer grasp and can be a superb tool for introducing early math skills to your child. Like those on an abacus, the beads on this toy are fun to slide, but they can also be used to learn counting and preliminary addition and subtraction. Introduce concepts like "all," "none," and "some," action words like "move" and "slide" or directional words like "left," "right," "up," or "down" as your child moves the beads.

Ruler

Precision crafting knife

Cardboard

Pencil

Pushpin

3 (12" [30-cm]) pipe cleaners (also called chenille stems) in any colors

30 pony beads in any colors

Hot glue gun and glue

1. With the ruler and precision crafting knife, measure and cut 2 (8 x 10–inch [20 x 25–cm]) pieces of cardboard.

2. Measure 1½ inches (4 cm) from the top border of one piece of cardboard, and use the pencil to mark 2 holes that are 8 inches (20 cm) apart. Repeat this step for the bottom border, then mark 2 holes halfway between the top and bottom rows. Use the pushpin to make holes at each of the six marks.

3. Feed a pipe cleaner through the top-left hole, and fold the first 1½ inches (4 cm) of the pipe cleaner onto the back of the cardboard. Repeat this process for all 3 rows.

4. Thread 10 pony beads onto each pipe cleaner.

5. Feed the opposite ends of the pipe cleaners through the remaining holes and pull the pipe cleaners taut, then fold the ends onto the back of the cardboard.

6. Apply hot glue over the pipe cleaners' ends and the back of the cardboard, then adhere the second cardboard sheet so that the pipe cleaner ends are sandwiched between the cardboard. Your child is ready to slide and count!

# ▲ BAT-AND-PLAY RIBBON OCTOPUS ▲

This cute toy, ideal for tummy time and back play, will intrigue infants with color and movement and encourage them to develop motor skills and hand-eye coordination as they learn to bat and grasp the ribbons. Older babies and toddlers can use this toy for imaginative play and color recognition.

▲    ▲    ▲

Single hole punch

Plastic cup

8 (12" [30-cm]-long) ribbons in different colors

Lighter

Knife

1 (24" [60-cm]-long) ribbon in any color

Black permanent marker

Play gym

1. With the single hole punch, create 8 holes that are fairly evenly spaced along the top rim of the plastic cup.

2. Run the ends of each 12-inch (30-cm)-long ribbon quickly over the flame of a lighter to seal the ends of the ribbons and prevent them from fraying.

3. Thread 1 ribbon through each hole, and tie each ribbon to the cup with a double knot.

4. Poke a small hole in the bottom of the cup with a knife, and then thread the 24-inch (60-cm)-long ribbon through the hole. Tie a double knot inside the cup, then pull the ribbon through the cup so that the cup hangs upside down.

5. Draw eyes and a mouth on the cup with a black permanent marker to create the octopus's face.

6. Fold the top ribbon in half, then drape the folded ribbon over the bar of your baby's play gym. Feed the cup and end of the ribbon through the loop and pull the cup and the ribbon's end. The cup will hang from the play gym. Baby will enjoy staring at the octopus—and beginning around 3 months old, baby may be able to hit the ribbons if they are close to their hands. Older babies and toddlers will enjoy playing with the octopus and learning the colors of each ribbon.

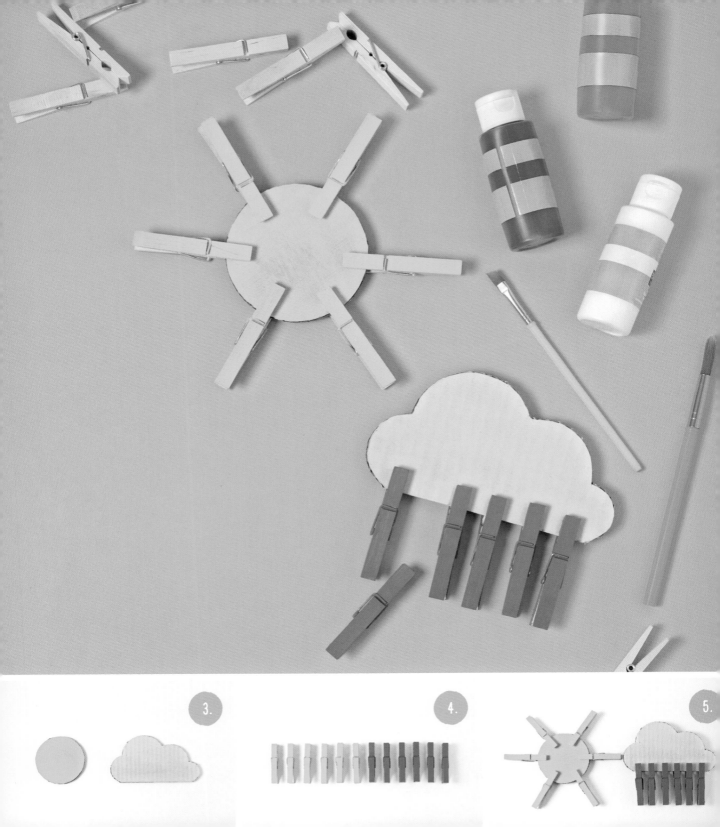

3.

4.

5.

# ▲ CLOTHESPIN SUN AND CLOUD ▲

Add a little sunshine to your child's day with this fine motor and color-matching challenge. Introduce the concept of weather to your toddler as well: Look outside. If it's raining, take out the rain cloud; if it's sunny, bring out the sun! Younger babies will focus on removing the clothespins, whereas older toddlers can work toward both removing and replacing them, which builds hand strength and precision.

Pencil

Large Circle Template (page 173)

Cloud Template (page 165)

White computer paper

Scissors

Cardboard

Precision crafting knife

Paintbrush and acrylic paint in yellow, blue and white

12 wooden clothespins

1. With a pencil, trace the Large Circle Template and Cloud Template onto sheets of white paper and cut them out with scissors. Then trace the cutouts onto a piece of cardboard.

2. Cut the shapes out with a precision crafting knife.

3. Paint the circle with the yellow acrylic paint, applying additional coats of paint as desired to coat the cardboard. Combine the blue and white paints to create light blue, then paint the cloud.

4. Paint the tops of 6 of the clothespins yellow. Paint the tops of the remaining 6 clothespins blue. When the paint is dry, flip the clothespins over and paint the bottoms. If desired, paint the clothespins' sides as well.

5. When the shapes and clothespins have fully dried, place the clothespin rays and raindrops on their corresponding shapes for your child to pull. Toddlers can attempt to place the clothespins on the shapes and match the colors.

# ▲ POUCH LID TRACKS ▲

This activity can help your child develop nimble hands and a nimble mind. Pushing or pulling the lids left and right takes focus and coordination, and you can introduce the concept of direction as your child plays. Inspire your toddler's imagination by suggesting the lids are switches on a rocket ship, or pretend the box is an oven with an on-off control–help them turn on the oven and put toy food inside. Add stickers to each side of the sliders, like a red dot and a green dot. The possibilities for this open-ended toy are limitless!

▲   ▲   ▲

Cardboard shoebox

Paintbrush and acrylic paint

Ruler

Pencil

Precision crafting knife

Cardboard

Hot glue gun and glue

2 empty snack pouches

Serrated knife

Masking tape (optional)

1. Paint the shoebox with the acrylic paint, applying multiple coats to cover the box.

2. When the paint has fully dried, use the ruler and pencil to measure and mark a ½-inch (1.3-cm)-wide slot on the top and long side of the box. Leave a minimum of 1 inch (2.5 cm) from the edge of the box on each side of the slot. Keep in mind that cutting more than 1 slot on any side will weaken the box, as will cutting a long slot on a large box— try making the slots on a small box like a kid's shoebox or keeping the slot short if the box is large.

3. Cut the slots out with a precision crafting knife.

4. Measure and cut out 4 (1¼-inch [3-cm]) squares from the cardboard. Hot-glue the squares together in pairs, one square on top of another.

5. Cut the necks and lids off each snack pouch with a serrated knife, right above the plastic pouch. Discard the plastic pouch and clean the lid and neck. Allow the lid and neck to dry completely before proceeding to the next step.

6. Hot-glue the bottom, flat portions of the pouch necks to the 2 cardboard squares.

7. Open the box and push the plastic necks through the slots, so that the cardboard squares are on the inside of the box.

8. Test whether the lids glide easily by screwing the lids onto the necks and sliding them back and forth. If there is too much friction, remove the lids and necks, then tape the edges of the slots with masking tape. Replace the necks and lids.

9. Apply a small amount of hot glue to the inside of the lids, then screw them tightly onto the necks. Allow the glue to dry completely. Let your child slide the lids left and right.

2.

5.

6.

7A.

7B.

8.

# DROP-AND-TWIST STATION

Is your child fascinated by container lids? Removing and replacing lids is a superb challenge for your baby or toddler, and this toy will give them a more stable base for twisting. If your baby is eating solids, try giving them baby puff snacks or O-shaped cereal to place into the container and dump. If your toddler is no longer mouthing objects, pom-poms are a fun, colorful option. Don't worry if your baby can't twist the lid on and off yet–they can start by placing the lid on and removing it, then graduate to screwing the lid on tightly.

Ruler

Precision crafting knife

Cardboard

Plastic sports drink bottle with a lid at least 1½" (4 cm) in diameter, washed and dried

Box cutter

Pencil

Paintbrush and acrylic paint (optional)

Hot glue gun and glue

Baby puff snacks or O-shaped cereal for younger babies or pom-poms for older toddlers

1. Using the ruler and precision crafting knife, measure and cut 3 (4 x 4–inch [10 x 10–cm]) squares from the cardboard.

2. Carefully cut the top portion of the sports drink bottle with a box cutter. Discard the bottom portion of the bottle.

3. With a pencil, trace the cut portion of the bottle onto 2 of the cardboard squares. Cut the circles out of the cardboard squares with the precision crafting knife.

4. If desired, use acrylic paint to coat one of the cardboard squares with a cutout hole. You can also paint the edges of all 3 of the squares if you would like. Trace one of the cut holes in the cardboard squares onto the third piece of cardboard and paint the circle—it is okay to paint outside of the lines.

5. When the paint is fully dry, hot-glue the 3 cardboard layers together, with the unpainted cardboard sheet between the fully painted top sheet and the bottom sheet with the painted circle.

6. Apply hot glue to the inside of the hole, around the rim of the hole only. Place the cut bottle into the hole and hold the bottle in place until the glue dries.

7. Once the glue has dried, add your preferred filling to the drop-and-twist station and let your little one enjoy!

# ▲ RIBBON COLANDER ▲

Your kitchen is a treasure trove of baby and toddler play materials! Pull out a colander for this activity–the setup is easy and, as long as you can go without your colander, you can leave this toy intact. Encourage prelanguage skills by making a repetitive noise like "woo" or "wee" each time baby pulls a ribbon, and let your baby try to imitate you. Grasping and pulling builds muscles and dexterity, and your toddler will love discovering how to flip the colander over and pull the ribbons through the other side. Try placing this in front of your infant during tummy time–the mirror-like reflection and colors will delight them.

Ruler

Scissors

Ribbons in rainbow colors

Lighter

Metal colander with large holes

1. With the ruler and scissors, measure and cut 8 (12-inch [30-cm]) lengths of ribbon. Cut the ribbon at an angle so that it comes to a point on each end.

2. Quickly run the ribbon over the flame of a lighter to seal the ends.

3. Thread each ribbon through a hole in the colander, then tie a double knot in the end of each ribbon on the inside of the colander.

4. Pull the ribbons to ensure the knots will not fit through the colander's holes, then tie a double knot on the opposite ends of the ribbons.

5. Pull the ribbons to the inside of the colander then flip the colander upside down. Baby can pull all the ribbons, then you can flip the colander over for them to pull the ribbons again; your toddler can flip it themselves.

# ENGAGING SENSORY PLAY

Babies and toddlers explore the world around them through their senses, and engaging their senses is crucial for brain development.[15] The projects in this chapter primarily focus on hearing, touch and sight to capture your child's interest and create lasting neural connections. Sensory exploration leads to sensory integration, the ability to receive information through one's senses then organize and use the information to properly interact with one's environment.[16] Sensory integration is important for developing motor skills, language and problem-solving ability, and it can even help your little one develop trust and be comfortable with a variety of experiences.[15] Set your child up with fun projects like the Rainbow Chickpea Shaker (page 102), Crinkle Square (page 97), Taste-Safe Sponge Painting (page 93) or Bead Squishy Bag (page 106) to delight and captivate them.

# TASTE-SAFE SPONGE PAINTING

Incorporate creativity and sensory play into your little artist's day with this taste-safe paint–and keep it in the refrigerator for up to four days to use multiple times! Sponge shapes are a great option for babies and toddlers–they offer a fine motor challenge that is developmentally appropriate and not as difficult as using paintbrushes. Here's a tip for painting with babies: Tape around cardstock with masking or painters' tape and adhere it to the table so your baby can paint without the paper slipping.

▲    ▲    ▲

1 cup (125 g) all-purpose flour (see step 1)

1 cup (128 g) cornstarch (see step 1)

Large baking pan

3 small mixing bowls

6 tbsp (108 g) table salt

Whisk

5 cups (1.2 L) water

Small pot

3 small heatproof bowls

Liquid food coloring in blue, green and red

3 small containers with lids

Small Heart, Small Circle, Small Diamond, Small Triangle and Small Square Templates (page 166)

White computer paper

Scissors

Permanent marker

2 unused dish sponges

Paper plate

Cardstock

1. Preheat the oven to 350°F (180°C). Spread the flour and cornstarch on the baking pan, being sure they are not touching. Bake on the oven's middle rack for 15 minutes. This is essential to kill any bacteria present in the flour and cornstarch in order to make the paint taste-safe.

2. Next, gather 3 small mixing bowls and add ¼ cup (31 g) of the flour and 2 tablespoons (36 g) of the salt to each one, whisking to combine. You can discard any remaining flour.

3. Bring the water to a boil in a small pot. Transfer 1 cup (240 ml) of the boiling water to each heatproof bowl, then add the food coloring: 20 drops of blue for the blue paint; 20 drops of green for the green paint; 4 drops of blue and 16 drops of red for the purple paint. Remove the boiling water from the heat.

4. Add each bowl of colored water to the flour and salt, and then whisk until each mixture is smooth. Add 4 tablespoons (32 g) of the cornstarch to each bowl and whisk well. You can discard any remaining cornstarch.

5. If the paint is too thick, add 1 tablespoon (15 ml) of the hot water at a time and mix until the paint is smooth and slightly runny. Pour the paint into a small container.

6. To make the sponge stamps, trace the Small Heart, Small Circle, Small Diamond, Small Triangle and Small Square Templates onto white paper and cut out the shapes with scissors. Then, using a permanent marker, trace the cutouts onto the sponges and cut them out with scissors.

7. When the paint has cooled, pour a small amount onto a plate and let your baby discover how to dip the shape stamps into the paint then apply it to the cardstock. If they need some help, dip the shapes for them. The food coloring should not stain surfaces or little hands, but if it does, water and soap will help remove the dye.

8. Refrigerate the paint within 2 hours of making it. To use it again, heat it in the microwave on high for 2 minutes, stirring it halfway through. If the paint thickens, thin it with 1 teaspoon of hot water at a time, mixing until you reach the desired consistency. Let the paint cool to room temperature before offering it to your child.

# TUBE SHAKERS

These easy-to-make shakers will engage your child in sensory play through sound. Your little one will love hearing these rattle as they shake or hit them. Introduce these musical instruments as a fun way to prolong back play, tummy time or side-lying play for infants or as maracas for older babies and toddlers to shake and explore. Older toddlers can even help decorate their own shakers!

▲ ▲ ▲

3 toilet paper tubes

Paintbrush and acrylic paint or child-safe markers (optional)

Hot glue gun and glue

¾ cup (150 g) uncooked rice

Scissors (optional)

Single hole punch

3 (24" [60-cm]-long) pieces of string

Play gym

1. If desired, paint the toilet paper tubes with acrylic paint, or let your child decorate them with markers.

2. When the paint has dried, hot-glue one end of each toilet paper tube to close it, applying the glue inside the end of the tube then pressing the edges of the tube together until the glue dries.

3. Pour approximately ⅛ cup (25 g) of uncooked rice into each tube. Hot-glue the other end of the tube and seal it by pinching together the open edges of the tube so that they are perpendicular to the glued end of the tube—the side of the shaker will appear triangular. If desired, use scissors to round out the corners of the shakers so they are less sharp.

4. Using the single hole punch, create a hole on one end of each roll, ensuring the hole stays within the glued portion so as not to release the rice.

5. Insert a piece of the string through the hole in each shaker and tie the string to your baby's play gym. Let the shakers hang at a height your baby can reach up to hit, but keep them out of the way of your baby's eyes. If you are using these as an instrument for an older baby or toddler, omit the string and set the shakers in a basket for your child to explore.

# CRINKLE SQUARE

Create this easy, no-sew lovey that crinkles and intrigues your baby as they play. Toddlers can use this as a blanket for stuffed animals and dolls or even as a musical instrument! Make it your own by adding as many ribbon loops as you would like for baby to grab and mouth, and try different colors or textures of ribbon to add an element of exploration. Infants will love hearing you crunch the soft square, and the ribbon loop can be attached to a play gym so that baby can lie or sit and grab the crinkle square.

Ruler

Permanent marker

2 (9 x 12" [23 x 30-cm]) sheets of soft felt in different colors

Scissors

Parchment paper

Hot glue gun and glue

1 (6" [15-cm]-long) ribbon, plus more if desired

1. Using the ruler and permanent marker, measure and mark a 8 x 8–inch (20 x 20–cm) square on each felt sheet. Cut out each square with the scissors.

2. Cut out a 7 x 7–inch (18 x 18–cm) piece of parchment paper. Apply hot glue around the edges of the parchment paper, then adhere it to one of the felt squares, centering it and leaving a 1-inch (2.5-cm) border of felt.

3. Apply hot glue to the end of the ribbon and adhere it to a corner of the felt and parchment paper. If desired, glue additional pieces of ribbon around the edge or at each corner.

4. Apply hot glue to the other end of the ribbon and fold the ribbon over to form a loop. Hold the ribbon in place until the hot glue is dry and secure.

5. Apply hot glue around the edge of the felt and over the ribbon, then place the second square of felt on top and press down until the hot glue is dry and secure. Let baby crunch, crinkle and shake away!

# ▲ OCEAN BOTTLE ▲

Create a soothing sensory bottle to engage baby or to use as a calming tool for toddlers. This simple-to-make bottle uses marine elements and blue food coloring to create an ocean in a bottle, but you can create similar bottles with any theme you would like. Use red food coloring and red and white beads to make a candy cane bottle. Try green food coloring and flower-shaped beads or confetti for a spring theme. Sensory bottles can stimulate your baby's vision, intriguing them with motion as they roll the bottle or you roll the bottle for them. Toddlers can explore moving the bottle on their own, or you can use the bottle as a tool to teach them self-regulation. Have your child breathe and focus on the moving contents as a way to calm themselves.

12- to 20-oz (360- to 600-ml) clear plastic bottle with lid

Water

Liquid food coloring in blue

Baby oil or vegetable oil

Small ocean-themed items that fit through the bottle's mouth (such as toy animals, shells, erasers and confetti)

Hot glue gun and glue

1. Fill the plastic bottle one-third full with water. Add 1 drop of blue food coloring.

2. Fill the rest of the bottle with baby oil. If you substitute the baby oil with vegetable oil, keep in mind that the oil will not be clear.

3. Add a few of the ocean-themed items, like toy animals and shells.

4. Apply hot glue to the inside of the bottle's lid, then close the bottle and allow the glue to dry. This sensory bottle is great for tummy time or for older kids to explore! Try the same method with different shades of food coloring and different items to make different themes.

# BUTTON WATER MAT

Sensory water mats are a great way to incorporate touch and visual stimulation for baby while lengthening tummy time and making it a positive experience. Toddlers will also enjoy touching the bag and watching the buttons move. All you need to create your own is a gallon bag, water, tape and something to put in the bag—colorful buttons are a great choice. Try making multiple bags and putting other objects inside, like pom-poms, sequins, confetti, foam shapes, small plastic animals, small erasers or natural items like leaves or flowers.

Alcohol swab

1 (1-gallon [3.8-L]) plastic storage bag (preferably freezer-safe; see step 5 for older children)

50 medium-sized colorful buttons

7 cups (1.7 L) water

Duct tape (optional)

1. Using an alcohol swab, wipe the label off of the plastic storage bag.

2. Fill the bag with the buttons.

3. Add the water to the bag and close the bag, carefully squeezing the air out as you seal the bag. If needed, tape the bag's seal with duct tape to prevent leaks.

4. If your baby is unable to lift or bite the bag, they can play with the bag on the floor without the sides being taped down. For older babies, tape the bag down around the edges using the duct tape, first testing that the tape will not damage the floor.

5. Baby will enjoy touching the bag and watching the buttons move. If your baby isn't old enough to touch the bag themselves, move it for them so they can watch the buttons sway. Placing the water and buttons in a reusable silicone bag rather than a single-use plastic bag is a great way for older children to explore with less risk of breaking the bag.

# RAINBOW CHICKPEA SHAKER

Babies and toddlers learn through their senses. This colorful shaker makes a pleasing, attention-grabbing sound and will delight your child visually. If baby is learning to crawl, try slowly rolling the bottle just out of reach, then letting them make their way to it. Use the same method of dyeing chickpeas to make a sensory bin when your toddler is no longer mouthing objects. Put the dyed chickpeas and some scoops and cups in a large storage bin, and let your toddler play!

▲  ▲  ▲

1½ to 2 cups (300 to 400 g) dried chickpeas

12- to 20-oz (360- to 600-ml) clear plastic bottle with lid

Funnel

Measuring cup

6 plastic sandwich bags

3 to 4 tsp (15 to 20 ml) distilled white vinegar

Liquid food coloring in red, yellow, blue and green

Medium baking sheet

Hot glue gun and glue (optional)

1. Pour the chickpeas into the clean, dry plastic bottle with the help of the funnel. Leave a small amount of space for the chickpeas to rattle—too much space will make the rattle loud, so test the sound and add more chickpeas if necessary. Pour the chickpeas into a measuring cup to measure how many chickpeas fit in the bottle. A 12-ounce (360-ml) bottle should fit approximately 1½ cups (300 g) of dried chickpeas.

2. Divide the total amount of chickpeas by how many colors you would like to make for your bottle. To create a rainbow bottle, you will need 6 plastic sandwich bags. Divide the chickpeas evenly among the 6 bags; for example, if you are using a 12-ounce (360-ml) bottle and 1½ cups (300 g) of chickpeas, place ¼ cup (50 g) of chickpeas in each sandwich bag.

3. Add ½ teaspoon of vinegar per ¼ cup (50 g) of chickpeas, then close each bag and shake it so that the vinegar coats the chickpeas.

4. Add approximately 12 drops of liquid food coloring to each ¼ cup (50 g) of chickpeas: Use 12 drops each of red, yellow, blue and green to create those individual colors. To make orange chickpeas, use 2 drops of red and 10 drops of yellow. For purple chickpeas, use 10 drops of red and 2 drops of blue. Close the bag and shake it until the food coloring coats the chickpeas.

5. Pour the colored chickpeas onto the baking sheet. Leave them out at room temperature until they have fully dried, approximately 1 hour.

6. For a layered effect, pour one color of chickpeas into the plastic bottle at a time. If desired, hot-glue the inside of the bottle's lid, then twist the lid on and let the glue dry so that your child cannot remove the lid. Baby can shake, rattle and roll!

# TACTILE SENSORY PATH

Your baby may be used to exploring with their hands—give them a chance to explore different textures with their feet! Not only is this a great tactile sensory experience but it can also encourage gross motor activity like walking or crawling. Set up this sensory path on the floor on a rainy day to get your little one moving and investigating. If you want to make this a more permanent game, tape the items down to a large piece of cardboard and use it on top of a rug or carpet or over nonslip pads, then store it away and take it out again later!

2 (1-gallon [3.8-L]) plastic storage bags (preferably freezer-safe)

3 cups (540 g) dried split peas, beans or lentils

1 (20-oz [600-ml]) bottle of hair gel

Duct tape

Ruler

Scissors

Bubble Wrap®

1 (8½ x 11" [21 x 28–cm]) sheet of colored paper (optional)

1 (9 x 12" [23 x 30–cm]) sheet of stiff felt

Painters' tape

1. Fill 1 plastic storage bag with the split peas. Close the bag, letting the air out as you seal it.

2. Fill the remaining storage bag with the hair gel. Close the bag, letting the air out as you seal it. If the bag leaks, secure the seal with the duct tape.

3. With the ruler and scissors, measure and cut a piece of Bubble Wrap that is roughly 11 x 11 inches (28 x 28 cm). If desired, place the colored paper under the Bubble Wrap to add color.

4. Line up the Bubble Wrap, filled storage bags and the felt on a hard, bare floor. Starting on one side, tape the sides of the materials or bags down to the floor with painters' tape or additional duct tape, first testing that the tape does not damage the floor's surface. When taping the filled bags, push the contents toward the center of the bags, then apply the tape.

5. Tape the tops and bottoms of the materials to the floor. Ensure the tape is secure.

6. Allow your baby to explore touching, standing, walking and crawling on the materials. Try out any other safe materials you have at home as well.

# ▲ BEAD SQUISHY BAG ▲

Squishy bags are a fun way to incorporate sensory play into your child's routine without making a mess. This is a great activity for babies who have recently discovered their hands and are beginning to feel and explore different sensations during tummy time. Setting the bag in front of baby while they play in a seated position is also a wonderful way to encourage sitting independently–you can even tape the bag to a vertical surface, like a low window or the wall, to encourage wrist extension, shoulder stability and core strength. To use this as a sorting bag for an older toddler, draw colored circles on the bag with permanent markers–your child can move the beads around in the gel to sort them into the correct circles.

▲    ▲    ▲

Alcohol swab

1 (1-gallon [3.8-L]) plastic storage bag (preferably freezer-safe)

1 cup (240 g) pony beads

1 (20-oz [600-ml]) bottle of hair gel

Duct tape

Painters' tape (optional)

1. Use an alcohol swab to remove the label from the plastic storage bag.

2. Fill the bag with the pony beads. You can also try other fillers, like confetti, small plastic animals or small erasers.

3. Add the hair gel to the bag and close the bag, carefully squeezing out the air as you seal the bag.

4. If the bag leaks, tape the seal with the duct tape.

5. Baby can play with the bag on the floor without the sides taped down if they are unable to lift or bite the bag. For older babies, tape the bag around the edges using the painters' tape or additional duct tape and secure it to the wall or floor, ensuring the tape does not damage any surfaces.

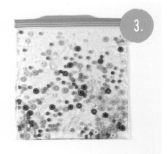

# CAKE TIN DRUM

This drum is a fun way to upcycle your single-use cake or pie tins. Your child will love to experiment with cause and effect, banging and shaking in their one-baby band. Young babies can listen to you rattle the drum and watch light reflect off the tins. Complete your recycled instrument set with rubber bands over an empty tissue box—a rubber band guitar!—and a shaker like the Rainbow Chickpea Shaker (page 102) or a plastic bottle filled with small bells or beads.

¼ cup (50 g) uncooked rice

2 foil cake or pie tins in matching sizes

Hot glue gun and glue

1. Pour the rice into one of the cake or pie tins.

2. Apply hot glue generously around the rim of the tin.

3. Place the remaining cake or pie tin on top, lining up the rims carefully and holding the tins in place until the hot glue sets. Apply additional hot glue around the rim of the tins as necessary to fully seal the drum.

4. When the hot glue has fully dried, allow your child to bang and shake away.

# NATURAL SENSORY LIDS

Place these textured lids in front of baby during tummy time or while they are sitting, and let them reach, feel and observe. Baby can explore touching different natural items with less risk of placing the objects in their mouth. These lids can also be a fun way to gather items and practice counting with your toddler! Use a basket to collect rocks, pine cones and nuts or other items outside, then count with your child to see how many of each item fit on a lid.

▲  ▲  ▲

3 (4" [10-cm]) plastic canister lids

Natural materials (such as small rocks, sticks, nuts, pieces of bark, shells or pine cones)

Precision crafting knife

Hot glue gun and glue

1. Wash and dry the plastic canister lids. Lids from raisin or cocoa powder canisters work well for this project.

2. Collect natural items such as small rocks, sticks, nuts, pieces of bark, shells or pine cones. Clean any dirty objects, and allow them to dry if necessary.

3. Using a precision crafting knife, lightly score the whole surface of the inside of the lids. Scoring the plastic helps ensure the items do not come loose later.

4. Working from the top of the lids downward, hot-glue the natural materials to the inside of the lids. As the glue dries, check that the items are secured well.

5. Try placing the lids in front of your baby one at a time so they can explore.

# VISUAL EXPLORATION

Vision is a vital sense for exploration as babies and toddlers learn more about the world. Babies' play in the first four months of life is highly visual, as they develop depth perception, the ability to see colors and the ability to track objects with their eyes. During the next few months, babies start to coordinate their hand movements with their vision, grabbing objects and focusing their eyes with more precision. Around eight to twelve months old, babies become mobile and use their eyes to judge distance and orient themselves.[17] They also develop object permanence, the understanding that hidden objects still exist.[18] Older babies and toddlers will continually grow and explore through all their senses, especially sight, as they hone their coordination. The projects in this chapter—like the Black-and-White Montessori Mobile (page 120), Rainbow Spinner (page 127) and "I Spy" Bottle (page 116)— are vision-focused and promote hand-eye coordination, tracking and improved perception.

# EMOTION-CHANGING FACE

Create this fun face to help your child develop emotional intelligence and fine motor skills. As you and baby move the face components, you can talk about the emotions the face is expressing. Your child will have fun trying to turn the pieces and eventually conveying their own emotions on the face. You can even use this as a tummy time prop—babies are intrigued by faces!

Pencil

8" (20-cm) plate

Cardboard

Precision crafting knife

Face Component Templates (page 166)

White computer paper

Scissors

Paintbrush and acrylic paint in black, white, brown and pink

Brad paper fasteners

Hot glue gun and glue

1. Using the pencil, trace around the plate on the cardboard. Cut out the circle with the precision crafting knife.

2. Trace the Face Component Templates onto the white paper and cut them out with scissors. Then trace the cutouts onto another piece of cardboard and cut them out with the precision crafting knife. For the eyes, first trace and cut out 2 eyes. Cut out the iris circle from the template, and then trace around it on the cardboard eyes. This will be a guide for painting the iris. Trace and cut out 2 eyebrows, 1 nose and 1 mouth.

3. Paint the eyes, eyebrows, nose and mouth in the appropriate colors with the acrylic paint. If desired, paint the tops of the brad paper fasteners to match the colors of the face components.

4. To assemble the face, use the precision crafting knife to cut a small slit in the middle of each face component and insert a brad through each hole. If you painted the tops of the brads, make sure each one is matched with its corresponding face component. Then use the precision crafting knife to cut a small slit on the large circle where you will attach each face component. Ensure that the components will have space to turn. Insert the brads through the slits in the large circle.

5. Open the backs of the brads and reinforce them with hot glue so they cannot be removed.

6. When the hot glue has dried, spin each face component so that it moves easily. Let your child move the pieces to create different facial expressions.

# "I SPY" BOTTLE

This creative sensory bottle can be used in many ways—as an investigative game for older babies and toddlers, a focal point during tummy time, a shaker or a roller. Your little one can shake and rotate this bottle to see various hidden items. Use this as a fun opportunity for language development for older babies and toddlers; for example, say, "I spy a yellow sun," and then encourage your toddler to search for the sun by rotating and shaking the bottle. If your toddler is no longer mouthing, you can also pour the contents of the bottle in a bin and allow your child to hide and find the objects in the rice while you supervise.

12- to 20-oz (360- to 600-ml) clear plastic bottle with a lid

¼-cup (50-g) measuring cup

Small colorful items that fit through the bottle's mouth (such as toy animals, beads, erasers, dice, sequins or mini plastic building blocks)

Funnel

1 to 2 cups (200 to 400 g) uncooked rice

Hot glue gun and glue (optional)

1. Clean and dry a plastic bottle and its lid. Ensure there is no residual moisture in the bottle or lid.

2. Fill the measuring cup with the small colorful items. Pour the items into the empty bottle.

3. Insert a funnel into the bottle's mouth. Add the uncooked rice, ¼ cup (50 g) at a time. After adding each ¼ cup (50 g) of rice, shake and rotate the bottle gently so the items mix in with the rice. Continue adding rice until the bottle is mostly full but there is enough empty space to allow the contents to move around when the bottle is shaken.

4. If desired, hot-glue the bottle lid onto the bottle by applying a small amount of glue to the inside of the lid, then twisting it onto the bottle. Allow the glue to dry completely.

5. Set the bottle out for your child to shake, roll and observe during tummy time or seated play!

# PEEKABOO BOARD

This board will fascinate your child, introducing object permanence and promoting both fine and gross motor skills. Place the board in front of baby during tummy time or while they are sitting, and let them reach for and grab the flaps. Or help baby by opening the flaps to reveal the images if your child is not yet able to grasp. Infants will love the black, white and red shapes, and older babies and toddlers will enjoy hiding and finding each picture. Create different images to switch it up, or let your toddler help you draw the images to hide.

▲   ▲   ▲

Pencil

Leaf Template (page 167)

Insect Templates (page 167)

White computer paper

Scissors

Black permanent marker

1 (9 x 12" [23 x 30-cm]) sheet of soft green felt

1 (8½ x 11" [21 x 28-cm]) sheet of white cardstock, plus more if desired

Red permanent marker

Cardboard

1 clear plastic sheet protector for 8½ x 11" (21 x 28-cm) paper

Hot glue gun and glue

1. Using the pencil, trace the Leaf Template and Insect Templates onto the white paper and cut them out with scissors. Using the black permanent marker, lightly trace the left and right sides of the leaf cutout onto the center of the felt to make the middle leaf. Trace a leaf on each side of the middle leaf, with roughly ¾ inch (2 cm) of space between the leaves.

2. With the scissors, cut a slit at the bottom of each leaf to start cutting the sides of the leaves. Cut the leaves' sides, but keep the bases intact to form flaps.

3. Put the sheet of cardstock under the felt sheet, and use the pencil to trace the 3 leaf outlines onto the cardstock.

4. Within the outlines of each leaf, on the cardstock, trace 1 of the insect cutouts. Color the insects and draw any desired details with black and red permanent markers. If desired, trace the leaves onto additional sheets of cardstock and draw your own images; or print images, cut them out and glue them within the leaf outlines.

5. Trace the felt sheet onto cardboard and cut out the rectangle. Cut the binder holes off of the sheet protector. With the hot glue gun on low heat, apply hot glue around the edge of the sheet protector, then adhere it to the cardboard sheet, making sure that the sheet protector's opening faces the right-hand side of the cardboard.

6. Put the decorated cardstock in the sheet protector. Apply hot glue to the side of the felt that will be adhered to the sheet protector, but do not add glue to the backs of the leaves. Carefully press the felt, glued side down, over the sheet protector and align the leaves with the drawings on the cardstock. Ensure that the opening to the sheet protector remains open.

7. Add hot glue where necessary to ensure the felt stays in place. Your child can lift and close the flaps to cover and reveal each drawing, or you can prop the board in front of baby during tummy time with the images visible. If you want, you can switch out the cardstock so your child can reveal new drawings.

# BLACK-AND-WHITE MONTESSORI MOBILE

These gently spinning geometric shapes are superb for developing infants' visual perception.[18] Infants stare the longest at high-contrast images and faces, and during the first several months of life they will begin to track moving objects.[17] Use this mobile during back, side or tummy playtime, or hang it over baby's changing table–ensure that it is 8 to 12 inches (20 to 30 cm) away from baby and out of their reach. Homemade mobiles are great for supervised use while your baby is awake. Your little one will develop focus and concentration as they gaze at the linear and circular forms.

▲ ▲ ▲

Pencil

White Shape Templates (page 165), plus Large Circle Template (page 173)

White computer paper

Scissors

Large sheet of white poster board

Precision crafting knife

Black Shape Templates (page 164)

2 (8½ x 11" [21 x 28-cm]) sheets of black cardstock

Rubber cement

3 yards (3 m) string

1 (12" [30-cm]-long) wooden dowel

Ceiling hook (optional)

Play gym (optional)

1. With the pencil, trace the White Shape Templates and Large Circle Template onto the white paper and cut them out with the scissors. Next, lightly trace the cutouts onto the poster board.

2. Using a precision crafting knife, cut each shape out of the poster board.

3. Trace the 6 Black Shape Templates onto the white paper, cut them out, then trace the cutouts onto the cardstock. Cut out the shapes with a precision crafting knife. Trace and cut out the triangle 4 times to create the large black shape.

4. Apply a thin layer of rubber cement to the back of the black shapes and to the respective white shapes, then adhere them together, using the image as a guide. Each white poster board shape has 2 sides, with 1 black cardstock shape for each side.

5. Use the scissors to cut 3 (12-inch [30-cm]-long) pieces of string. Cut a small hole at the top of each shape with a precision crafting knife and thread a piece of string through each hole.

6. Tie the strings to the dowel, spacing the shapes apart fairly evenly. Cut a 24-inch (60-cm) length of string and tie each end to the ends of the dowel. Pull the string up so that it forms a triangle, and tie a loop at the top.

7. If desired, attach the mobile to the ceiling with a ceiling hook and the remaining string. Alternatively, attach the mobile to baby's play gym and let your little one watch the shapes move.

# FARM ANIMAL SHADOW PUPPETS

Shadow puppets are a classic activity for good reason! They are wonderful for introducing language through storytelling or songs, and they are visually stimulating. Young babies will enjoy the contrast of light and dark, and older babies and toddlers will be intrigued by the concept of projecting an image onto a wall using just a puppet and light. Using physical puppets rather than making hand shadows is a great option for young children because they can more easily participate in creating the shadows. Use these puppets in a lit room as well—one fun way to extend this activity is to cut slits in a paper egg carton and encourage your child to place the sticks in the slits and then remove the puppets as well.

Pencil

Shadow Puppet Templates (pages 168–169)

White computer paper

Scissors

6 (8½ x 11" [21 x 28-cm]) sheets of cardstock in any color

Hot glue gun and glue

6 craft sticks in any color

Flashlight

1. Trace the Shadow Puppet Templates onto the white paper and cut them out with scissors. Fold each sheet of cardstock in half, then use a pencil to trace 1 shadow puppet cutout onto each sheet.

2. Use the scissors to cut along the outlines through both layers of cardstock, so that you have 2 copies of each animal. Separate the copies of each animal so that you can work with a single animal shape at a time.

3. Apply a small dot of hot glue to one end of a craft stick, then adhere the craft stick to the back of one copy of a cardstock animal, near the bottom of the animal. Repeat this process with the remaining craft sticks and animals.

4. Apply a thin layer of hot glue to the entire back of a card-stock animal and to the top of the craft stick, then adhere the matching cardstock animal to the back, so that the 2 copies are aligned. Repeat this gluing process for each animal.

5. Introduce the shadow puppets to your child in a dark or dim room by holding the flashlight up to the animals and showing their projection on a wall. Let your baby or toddler explore trying to touch the shadows, moving the puppets, and making the shadows larger or smaller by moving the flashlight. Tell a story using the puppets or sing a familiar song about animals; young babies who are not able to hold the puppets will enjoy observing and listening.

# COLORFUL POM-POM GARLANDS

A colorful mobile hanging above baby during diaper changes or back play will help your child develop visual discrimination and give them a beautiful object to watch. Full-color vision may begin to emerge around five months of age, and stimulating baby with this intriguing mobile beginning around the time they are six weeks old can help improve visual perception.[17] Keep this mobile out of reach, and when your baby is no longer interested in gazing at the garland, turn this rainbow craft into a nursery decoration.

▲  ▲  ▲

Ruler

Scissors

1½ yards (1.5 m) sewing thread

1½ yards (1.5 m) string, plus more for hanging

Sewing needle

12 (1½" [4-cm]) pom-poms in different colors

1 (12" [30-cm]-long) wooden dowel

Ceiling hook

1. With the ruler and scissors, measure and cut a 16-inch (40-cm), 14-inch (35-cm) and 12-inch (30-cm) length of sewing thread. Then measure and cut a 24-inch (60-cm) length of string.

2. Thread the sewing needle with the 16-inch (40-cm) length of thread, and tie a double knot at the end, trimming any excess thread past the knot with scissors.

3. Insert the needle through the middle of a pom-pom and pull the thread gently until the knot catches at the bottom of the pom-pom.

4. Tie a double knot approximately 2 inches (5 cm) above the top of the pom-pom, then thread the next pom-pom onto the strand until it catches on the knot. Repeat this process until the first garland has 5 pom-poms with 3 inches (8 cm) of excess thread above the top pom-pom.

5. Repeat the preceding steps for the 14-inch (35-cm) and 12-inch (30-cm) lengths of thread, securing 4 pom-poms on the 14-inch (35-cm) thread and 3 pom-poms on the 12-inch (30-cm) thread.

6. Tie the ends of the 24-inch (60-cm) piece of string 1 inch (2.5 cm) inward from the ends of the dowel.

7. Tie the ends of the pom-pom garlands onto the dowel. Move them horizontally until the dowel hangs roughly level.

8. Tie the middle of the string into a loop. Attach an additional length of string to an installed ceiling hook, then tie the loop to the string so the bottom pom-pom hangs 8 inches (20 cm) above your baby's eye level. If your baby is reaching and grabbing, hang the mobile so that all of its pieces are out of reach. Never leave a homemade mobile over an area used for unsupervised sleep.

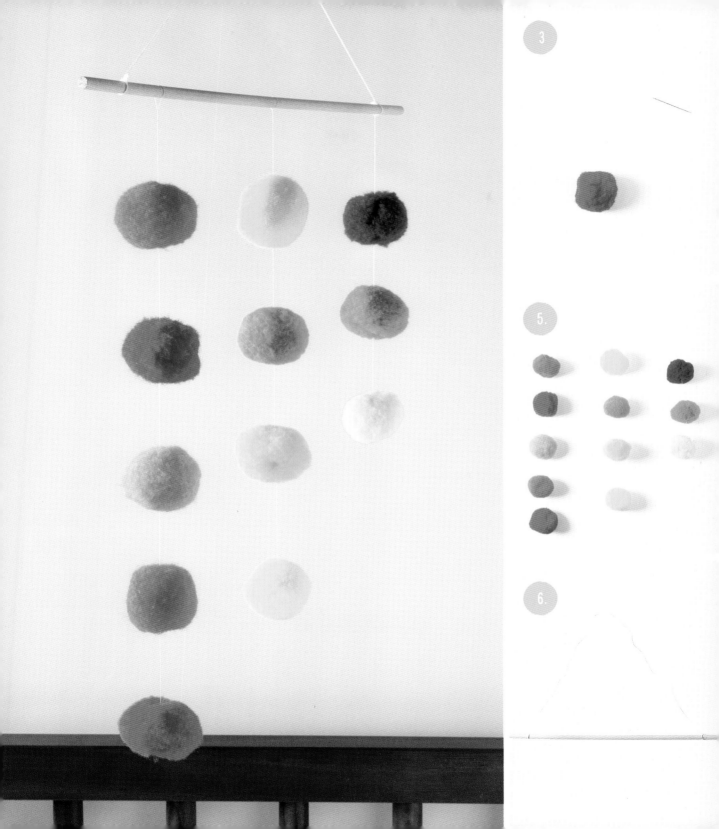

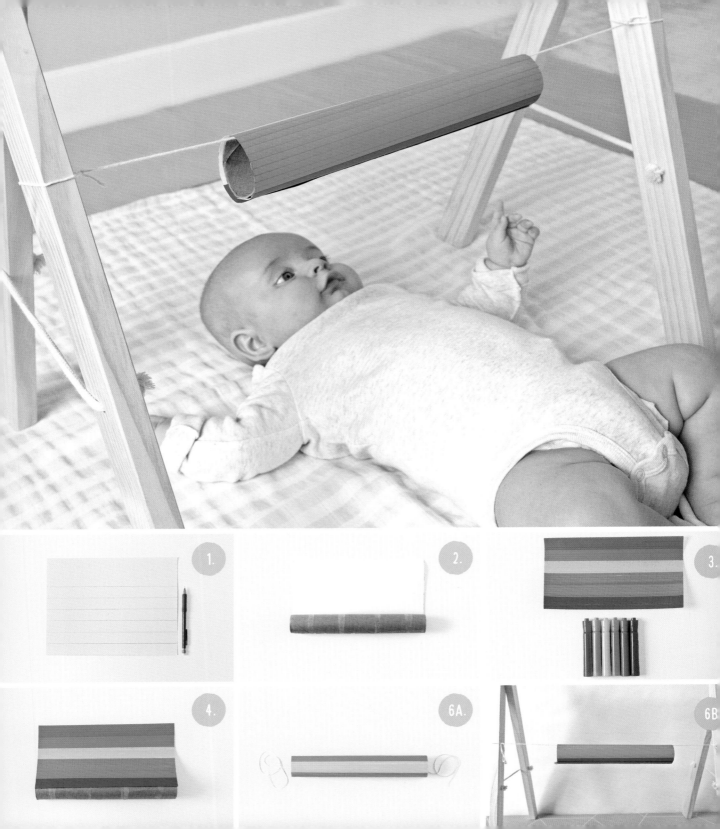

1.

2.

3.

4.

6A.

6B.

# RAINBOW SPINNER

This rainbow spinner will delight your baby, whether you spin it or baby is able to spin the roll independently. Using this toy will improve your baby's hand-eye coordination and help develop their vision–plus it is fun to hit! Every time your baby grabs or moves the roll, they will experience cause and effect, learning that moving their hand and hitting the spinner makes the colors change. Toddlers will have fun spinning the roll as fast as they can or pointing out and naming the colors. Use this roll in a new way by tying the string to high and low objects, then pulling the roll up and letting it slide down the string.

Ruler

Pencil

1 (8½ x 11" [21 x 28-cm]) sheet of white cardstock

Paper towel tube

Scissors

Chisel-tip poster markers in red, orange, yellow, green, blue and purple

Hot glue gun and glue

Clear packing tape (optional)

1 yard (1 m) string

Play gym or table legs

1. With the ruler and pencil, measure and mark 6 (1-inch [2.5-cm]) segments along the short sides of the cardstock. Use a ruler and pencil to lightly draw a line connecting each pair of markings to create each segment.

2. Test the fit of the cardstock around the paper towel tube, ensuring that the 6 segments will cover the roll. Adjust the last segment as necessary if more or less length is needed. Cut off the remaining portion of the paper with the scissors.

3. Color each segment with a different color marker. If desired, use the ruler as a guide to fill the segments with straight, uniform lines.

4. Apply a line of hot glue to the long edge of the back side of the cardstock, and adhere the cardstock to the paper towel tube. Continue to glue the cardstock around the tube, gluing 1 line at a time and rolling the cardstock onto the tube so that the cardstock lies flat.

5. If desired, cover the paper with long strips of clear packing tape and fold the ends inside the tube. This can be a helpful way to keep the spinner from getting wet if your child is likely to drool on it.

6. Cut a piece of string long enough to stretch between the legs of a play gym or a set of sturdy table legs. Thread the spinner onto the string and tie an end to each leg so the string is taut and the colorful tube can be easily spun. Your child can sit and lean forward to spin the roll, lie under it within reach and spin it or you can spin the tube for your baby to watch if they are not yet reaching for items.

# PLAYING CARD GALLERY

Create a high-contrast display to enhance tummy time or supervised time in the car. Hang the gallery in front of baby in the car, out of reach on the back of the seat to occupy baby on long drives–they will love staring at the high-contrast images. Use this craft for older babies as well– they will be challenged by pulling the cards out of the pockets and putting them back. Switch the cards out with photographs of family, cutouts from magazines or printed images.

Ruler

Pencil

Cardboard

Precision crafting knife

Paintbrush and black acrylic paint

1 (9 x 12" [23 x 30-cm]) sheet of soft red felt

Scissors

6 standard-sized playing cards

Permanent marker

1 clear plastic sheet protector for 8½ x 11" (21 x 28-cm) paper

Hot glue gun and glue

Single hole punch

1 yard (1 m) string

1. With the ruler and pencil, measure and mark an 11 x 13½–inch (28 x 34–cm) section of cardboard. Cut out the piece of cardboard using a precision crafting knife.

2. Paint the cardboard black and allow the paint to dry, using multiple coats if necessary.

3. Cut the felt in half lengthwise with scissors. Lay 3 of the playing cards on each piece of felt, spacing them evenly, and trace around them with a permanent marker. Cut the 6 rectangles out of the felt. You can discard the 6 cutout rectangles.

4. Cut the sheet protector in half, so that there are 2 single-layer pieces. Then cut one of the pieces in half lengthwise and discard the remaining pieces of sheet protector. With the hot glue gun on low heat, glue 1 plastic sheet to the back of each piece of felt.

5. Apply hot glue to the back of both felt sheets, leaving the area above each cutout rectangle free of glue to form pockets for the cards. Adhere the felt to the painted cardboard.

6. Punch 2 holes at the top of the cardboard and tie the ends of the string through the holes.

7. Hang the gallery over the back of the car's headrest opposite baby's car seat to use while closely supervised, or prop the cardboard in front of your child during tummy time.

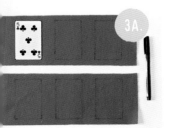

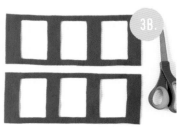

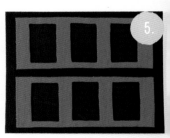

# NATURE MOBILE

Creating this nature mobile is simple and practically free, and observing these natural elements can soothe and intrigue your baby. Natural materials are calming and feature varying colors, textures and contrasts. A mobile over a changing pad or hung in front of your baby during playtime can help develop their vision and even encourage them to spend more time playing on their stomach, side or back. A great way to continue to use this mobile as your baby gets older is to let your child collect items on walks and help you switch out the items. Display the mobile on your child's wall or over their changing table, and talk about the items you have found.

3 natural items (such as craft feathers, dried flowers, small pine cones, dry leaves or pieces of bark)

Ruler

Scissors

2 yards (2 m) string or fishing line

1 (approximately 12" [30-cm]-long) dry stick measuring ¼ to ½" (6 mm to 1.3 cm) in diameter

Small ceiling hook

1. Gather 3 natural items. Allow the items to dry, if necessary, by setting them out or hanging them in a well-ventilated area until they are no longer damp to the touch. Brush off any debris.

2. Using the ruler and scissors, measure and cut 3 (8-inch [20-cm]) pieces of string and securely tie 1 string to each natural item.

3. Tie the opposite ends of the strings to the stick and double-knot the string. Evenly space the items and ensure the mobile can be hung level.

4. Cut a 36-inch (90-cm) piece of string and securely tie one end to each end of the stick wherever the strings can be easily attached and the stick hung balanced.

5. Tie a loop in the middle of the top string. Tie an additional length of string to an installed ceiling hook above your baby's play space or changing pad (not over your baby's unsupervised sleep space), high enough that the mobile is within your baby's vision but out of reach: 12 to 24 inches (30 to 60 cm). This mobile will be interesting enough to keep your infant's attention without being overstimulating— try placing your baby on their stomach with the mobile visible, or on their side with a towel rolled up behind them.

# MATCHING ANIMAL CARDS

Create a set of matching animal and shape cards to use as a memory game, a tummy time activity or an opportunity for independent exploration. Colorful cards can keep baby's attention and gaze, so set them out for an infant to observe or for an older baby to hold and investigate. These cards are a great way to encourage language development as you talk with your child about the animals and the sounds they make, as well as the shapes and their colors. Toddlers can use these cards to match the animal and shape pairs.

Pencil

Animal Card Templates (page 169)

Small Oval, Small Circle, Small Diamond, Small Triangle, Small Square and Small Star Templates (page 166)

White computer paper

Scissors

6 (8½ x 11" [21 x 28-cm]) sheets of cardstock in rainbow colors

12 (4 x 6" [10 x 15-cm]) blank index cards

Glue stick

Clear packing tape

1. Trace all of the Animal Card Templates and shape templates onto the white paper and cut them out with the scissors. Fold each sheet of cardstock in half. Use the pencil to trace 1 Animal Card cutout and 1 shape cutout—the Small Oval, Small Circle, Small Diamond, Small Triangle, Small Square or Small Star—onto each sheet.

2. Use the scissors to cut along the outlines through both layers of cardstock, so that you have 2 copies of each animal and shape; for example, 2 red monkeys and 2 red squares.

3. Glue each shape to an individual index card with a glue stick. On the back of each shape card, glue an animal of the same color. For example, glue the red monkeys on the back of the cards with the red squares.

4. Lay out a piece of packing tape with the sticky side facing upward, then overlap the tape with another piece of packing tape, sticky side up, by about ¼ inch (6 mm).

5. Place 1 animal/shape card down on the tape, leaving at least ¼ inch (6 mm) of tape around all the edges.

6. Place 2 more pieces of tape over the card, overlapped about ¼ inch (6 mm), so the entire card is covered in tape. Alternatively, use a laminating machine or self-sealing laminating pouches.

7. Cut around each card, leaving ⅛ inch (3 mm) of tape around the edges and rounding the corners of the tape.

8. Play a game with your child, encouraging them to find the matching card to the card you are holding. For babies, set the cards out and let them explore, or introduce the names of the animals and the sounds they make or the colors of the animals and shapes. For infants, prop a few cards up during tummy time to encourage them to push up on their arms to see the images.

# NOSTALGIC CD MOBILE

This throwback mobile can hang above your baby during diaper changes or back play to catch light and intrigue your child. This mobile is an easy way to upcycle CDs or DVDs you have held onto but no longer use while also helping your baby develop their visual discrimination and perception. The disks act as shiny mirrors that move gently and reflect baby's image and surroundings. When baby is older, use this craft as a nostalgic nursery decoration featuring your favorite bands or movies.

Pencil

Small Circle Template (page 166)

White computer paper

Scissors

4 (8½ x 11" [21 x 28-cm]) sheets of cardstock in yellow, light green, dark green and dark blue

Needle or pushpin

Thread in yellow, light green, dark green, dark blue and light blue (or colors of choice)

4 CDs or DVDs

Hot glue gun and glue

2 (12" [30-cm]-long) wooden dowels

String

Ceiling hook

1. Trace the Small Circle Template onto the white paper and cut it out with scissors. Then, trace the cutout onto the cardstock 8 times, drawing 2 circles on each sheet. Cut these out.

2. Using a needle, poke a small hole in the middle of each circle. In 1 circle of each color, cut a slit from one edge to the middle of the circle.

3. Cut a 6-inch (15-cm) length of yellow thread, an 8-inch (20-cm) length of light green thread, an 8-inch (20-cm) length of dark green thread and a 10-inch (25-cm) length of dark blue thread. Cut a 24-inch (60-cm) and a 28-inch (70-cm) length of light blue thread for hanging the dowel.

4. Thread the needle with the yellow thread and pass it through the hole in the yellow circle without the slit, then tie it off with a double knot. Repeat with the other 3 colors, matching the thread's color to the circle's color. Pull one of the threads up through one of the CD's center holes. Repeat with the remaining CDs.

5. Place the circles with slits around the strings on top of the CDs and overlap the edges to form cones. Mark the edge of each cone with a pencil—the cone should fit inside the inner ring of the CD.

6. Apply hot glue between the slit and your pencil mark, then overlap the edge to form a cone. To level the CD when it is hanging, pull the cone down gently so it rests in the inner ring of the CD and the CD is parallel to the floor.

7. Double-knot the thread above each cone. Tie the ends of the 24-inch (60-cm) piece of light blue thread to the ends of one of the dowels. Repeat this process with the 28-inch (70-cm) piece of light blue thread and the remaining dowel.

8. Tie the yellow CD and one of the green CDs to the dowel that has the shorter light blue string. Tie the other 2 CDs to the remaining dowel.

9. Cross the dowels, then tie the middle of the 2 top threads into a loop to join them. Adjust the CDs' threads to level the mobile. Tie the loop to a length of string attached to a ceiling hook to hang the mobile.

# IMAGINATIVE AND DRAMATIC PLAY

Imaginative play is beneficial for your child in numerous ways—it promotes problem-solving, empathy, curiosity and creativity, and it provides opportunities to develop language and social skills.[13] Your baby will begin by playing with items in straightforward ways, like feeding a baby doll from a pretend bottle or putting a teddy bear to sleep under a blanket. Then, your child will show symbolic thinking by pretending a block is a table for figurines or a banana is a telephone. Your child will move on to more dramatic play as they mature, creating story lines with toys and imagination. The following projects—like the Baby-Sock Finger Puppets (page 148), Felt Animal Masks (page 151), Rhythmic Rainstick (page 160) and Make-Believe Mailbox (page 141)—will inspire inventive and representational thinking.

Don't let your single socks go to waste! Create adorable sensory friends for squishing and storytelling. These precious bunnies can be attached to a play gym for baby to bat, placed in front of baby to grab or used in imaginative play. Make full-sized bunnies with adult socks or mini bunnies with baby socks. If you prefer, sew the bunnies' eyes and noses, or make this a no-sew craft by drawing the faces with permanent or fabric markers. Set a bunny or two out with toy carrots and create a cardboard rabbit house; your child benefits from creative pretend play!

## SOCK BUNNY

¾ cup (150 g) uncooked rice, divided

Long, thin adult dress sock in a solid color (such as gray, white, brown or tan)

Ruler

Scissors

16" (40 cm) string

12" (30 cm) fabric ribbon measuring ¾ to 1¼" (2 to 3 cm) wide

Lighter

Permanent marker or fabric marker

Needle and thread (optional)

1. Add ½ cup (100 g) of the rice to the sock.

2. With the ruler and scissors, measure and cut an 8-inch (20-cm) length of string and double-knot the string tightly above the rice to form the bottom part of the bunny. Pull the top of the sock up and out to remove some of the slack material. Cut the string ends so that they are ¼ inch (6 mm) long.

3. Cut a 10-inch (25-cm) length of ribbon. Tie the ribbon in a knot over the string, then cut the ends into a curve, leaving about a 1-inch (2.5-cm)-long tail on each side. Carefully and quickly, run the ends of the ribbon over the flame of a lighter to seal the ribbon and prevent it from fraying.

4. Add the remaining ¼ cup (50 g) of rice to the sock.

5. If you will be sewing the bunny's face, lightly mark the locations of the eyes and nose with a permanent or fabric marker, then remove the rice. Sew the face on with a needle and thread. Knot the thread and cut the ends, then add the rice back to the bunny. If you are drawing the bunny's face with the marker, leave the rice in the sock and proceed to the next step.

6. Tie an 8-inch (20-cm)-long string around the sock on top of the rice to form the bunny's head. Double-knot the string and cut the string ends so that they are ¼ inch (6 mm) long, or leave the string long if you intend to hang the bunny from baby's play gym for them to bat.

7. If you are drawing the bunny's face rather than sewing, use a black marker (if the sock is a light color) or a metallic silver marker (if the sock is a dark color) to draw 2 circles for eyes and a Y-shaped nose.

8. From the top portion of the sock, cut 2 semicircular bunny ears that come to a point at their ends and meet at the middle of the bunny's head to form a V. Discard the excess fabric.

(continued)

## BUNNY HOME AND CARROTS (OPTIONAL)

Pencil

10" (25-cm) round plate

Cardboard

Ruler

Precision crafting knife

Hot glue gun and glue

Paintbrush and acrylic paint in orange and green

6 to 7" (15- to 18-cm) round paper plate

Scissors

9. To create the optional bunny home, use the pencil to trace the 10-inch (25-cm) plate onto the cardboard. Using the ruler for guidance, draw a line through the middle of the circle to create 2 semicircles. Cut out the 2 (10-inch [25-cm]-diameter) cardboard semicircles with a precision crafting knife, and cut out doors and windows from 1 semicircle. For the roof, cut 17 strips of cardboard that are 1 inch (2.5 cm) wide and 6 inches (15 cm) long. Cut a 5 x 10–inch (13 x 25–cm) cardboard rectangle for the base. Hot-glue the semicircles t'o the rectangular base, and hot-glue the strips on top to form the roof.

10. To create the optional carrots, paint the bottom of the paper plate with the acrylic paint: Paint the rim green and the interior orange. Using scissors, cut the plate into 3 roughly equal segments. Overlap and hot-glue the ends to form cones. Cut slits in the green rims to form the carrot tops. Let your baby or toddler play and imagine!

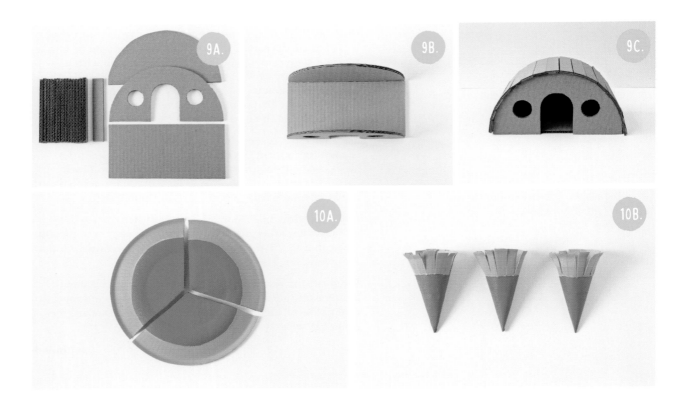

# MAKE-BELIEVE MAILBOX

Turn a package into a make-believe mailbox with durable envelopes for your child to "send." Posting objects is a favorite pastime for babies and toddlers–putting the letters in the box and closing the door is a great way to play. Toddlers can work on the sequence of opening the door, putting a letter inside, closing the door and raising the flag. Then they can act as the mail carrier by opening the door, removing the letter, closing the door and then lowering the flag. Practicing such a lengthy sequence of events is a fun way to play with your child and also teaches them pattern recognition. Add language acquisition for your baby or toddler by saying, "Open" each time you or your child opens the door. Then, when you find a letter, exclaim, "Wow, a letter!" Finally, as you shut the mailbox door, say, "Close!"

Small cardboard box

Paintbrush and acrylic paint in 2 colors

Pencil

Cardboard

Precision crafting knife

Hot glue gun and glue

Ruler

Hook-and-loop fastener squares (such as VELCRO® Brand fasteners)

1. Paint the cardboard box with 1 color of acrylic paint, leaving the top flaps unpainted. Painting over labels and removed tape can be difficult; instead, create a new top by using a pencil to trace the top of the box onto another sheet of cardboard and cutting out the new top with the precision crafting knife. Paint the new top to match the rest of the mailbox, and allow the paint to fully dry.

2. With the precision crafting knife, cut the top flaps off of the box, and adhere the new top with hot glue.

3. To make the mailbox's door, choose one end of the box and cut the top edge and side edges with a precision crafting knife. Leave the bottom edge intact so that it forms a flap.

4. With the ruler and pencil, measure and mark 2 (1 x 1¾–inch [2.5 x 4.5–cm]) pieces of cardboard; 1 (1 x 1–inch [2.5 x 2.5–cm]) piece of cardboard; and 1 (1 x 1½–inch [2.5 x 4–cm]) piece of cardboard. Cut out all of the pieces. Hot-glue the 2 (1 x 1¾–inch [2.5 x 4–cm]) pieces together, one on top of the other. Then hot-glue the remaining 2 pieces into an L shape, with the 1 x 1½–inch (2.5 x 4–cm) piece forming the vertical section of the L shape.

5. Hot-glue the hook side of a hook-and-loop fastener square to the double-layer cardboard piece and the loop side to the long side of the L-shaped piece. Paint the cardboard pieces with the other color of acrylic paint.

6. Apply hot glue to the unpainted sides of the pieces. Adhere the flat piece to the box's flap and the L-shaped piece to the inside of the box's opening, so that the pieces form the mailbox closure.

(continued)

6.

7.

8.

9.

Mailbox Flag Template (page 167)

White computer paper

Scissors

Brad paper fastener

1 (4¾ x 6½" [12 x 16.5-cm] or smaller) envelope

Permanent marker

6 (9 x 12" [23 x 30-cm]) sheets of stiff felt in different colors

1 (4½ x 6¼" [11 x 16-cm] or smaller) card

Clothes iron

7. Trace the Mailbox Flag Template onto the white paper, then cut it out with scissors. Trace the flag cutout onto cardboard and cut the flag out with a precision crafting knife. Paint the flag with acrylic paint to match the mailbox's closure, and allow the paint to fully dry. Cut a small slit in the flag's arm and insert a brad paper fastener, then cut a small slit in the mailbox's side, close to the mailbox's door, and insert the brad's end. Open the brad's end, and apply hot glue to it to ensure the brad cannot be removed.

8. To make the felt cards and envelopes, disassemble a small envelope by carefully opening the glued sides. Using the permanent marker, trace around the envelope onto a sheet of stiff felt. Trace the outline of the card onto another sheet of stiff felt. Cut the card and envelope out with scissors or fabric shears. Cut out a small rectangular piece of felt to make a stamp. Repeat this process to create a total of 3 envelopes, 3 cards and 3 stamps.

9. Fold the cards, then use the clothes iron to iron them briefly on medium heat so that the felt stays flat—be careful not to iron the felt so long that it begins to melt. Fold the envelope flaps and iron them briefly, again making sure the felt does not begin to melt. Hot-glue the envelope flaps, leaving the top flap open, to form the felt envelopes. Apply hot glue to the top-right corner of the envelope and adhere a felt stamp.

10. To close the envelopes, fold the top flap inside the envelope. Let your child open the mailbox, post the letters and lift the mailbox's flag. This can be a great activity for standing play—place the mailbox on an elevated surface like a couch cushion or an upside-down laundry basket.

# SUPERB DOLL SWING

Acting out normal daily activities is an essential part of pretend play for babies and toddlers.[13] Eating, sleeping and playing are routines your child will want to rehearse with their favorite doll or stuffed animal. This play swing is a fun accessory to inspire your child's imagination. Moving the doll in and out of the swing is also a great way to develop hand-eye coordination. Make this craft your own by painting it any color and using any shade of felt you would like. Pair this doll swing with the Baby Doll Bathroom on page 156 for even more imaginative play!

Cardboard box measuring at least 13" (33 cm) tall with flaps at least 6" (15 cm) wide

Precision crafting knife

Ruler

Pencil

Hot glue gun and glue

Paintbrush and acrylic paint in any colors (optional)

Permanent marker

2 (9 x 12" [23 x 30-cm]) sheets of soft felt in 1 color

Scissors

4 yards (4 m) string

Play gym or ceiling hook

1. Break down the cardboard box, cutting open any tape with the precision crafting knife and opening any glued sides, so that the box lies flat. There should be 3 folded corners. If the box is turned so the corner folds are vertically oriented to you, then, choosing one of the folds, use the ruler to measure 6½ inches (16 cm) on the left side of the fold and 6½ inches (16 cm) on the right side of the fold. With the pencil, draw a vertical line for each measurement that runs the length of the box from top to bottom, including through the box flaps. Then cut along both lines, so that you have a 13-inch (33-cm)-wide segment; at this point, the length of this segment is however long your box is.

2. Cut what was the side of the box until it measures 13 inches (33 cm) deep, leaving 2 of the flap segments on one side attached and removing the other 2 flaps (see the first image on page 146). Cut the flaps 6 inches (15 cm) deep.

3. Flip the cardboard over, so that the flaps fold under the cardboard. Measure 6 inches (15 cm) from the edge of the box's side, scoring the cardboard down the middle (do not cut all the way through) and then folding the seam. Flip the cardboard back over—the flap should fold up.

4. Cut out a segment of the middle of the new flap that is the same width as the gap between the original 2 flaps. All 4 flaps should measure approximately 6 x 6 inches (15 x 15 cm).

5. Cut each flap into a 1-inch (2.5-cm)-wide L shape, leaving the flap attached to the box's side.

6. Cut a rectangle out of the middle of the cardboard, so that the remaining portion creates a 1-inch (2.5-cm) border.

(continued)

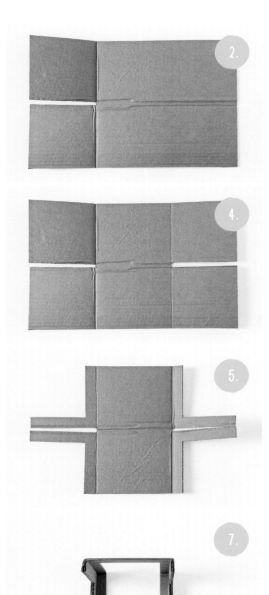

7. Fold the frame in the middle, then apply hot glue between the L-shapes and adhere them together. Allow the glue to dry, then paint the swing frame with the acrylic paint, if desired.

8. With the ruler and permanent marker, measure and mark 1 (4½ x 12–inch [11 x 30–cm]) piece and 2 (3½ x 4½–inch [9 x 11–cm]) pieces from 1 sheet of the felt. Cut out the pieces with the scissors. Cut the remaining felt sheet into a T shape, with the top arms of the T shape measuring 3½ inches (9 cm) wide and the stem of the T measuring 3 inches (8 cm) wide.

9. Hot-glue the 2 (3½ x 4½–inch [9 x 11–cm]) felt pieces to the arms of the T shape, overlapping them by ½ inch (1.3 cm). Hot-glue the 4½ x 12–inch (11 x 30–cm) felt piece to the top of the T shape, overlapping it by ½ inch (1.3 cm). The felt should form a cross.

10. To attach the felt to the swing frame, first hot-glue the narrow end of the cross to the front bar of the frame, then wrap the felt around the front bar.

11. Next, bring the arms of the cross around the sides of the swing frame, and hot-glue the ends to the inside and tops of the frame's sides.

12. Pull the wide top of the cross behind the swing, then up and over the top bar. Hot-glue the end to the back of the top bar.

13. Cut 4 (24-inch [60-cm]) lengths of string and tie them around the corners of the swing frame as shown in the photo. Pull the 4 strings together and tie the ends into a loop. Tie the swing onto a play gym, or hang another string from an anchored hook in the ceiling and attach it to the loop.

# BABY-SOCK FINGER PUPPETS

With just socks, markers and glue, you can make fun animal finger puppets for your child to enjoy. Tell stories, sing songs and play pretend with a fox, bird, bunny and bear. Hide the animal friends in Hide-and-Find Pouches (page 63) and play peekaboo. Take the puppets on an airplane or in the car—they are perfect, compact travel toys. Inspire your child's creativity by setting the animals out with block "caves" and "nests," and toy food, or cut a hole in a shoebox and pretend it is a hollow tree. The only limit is your imagination!

Permanent markers or fabric markers

Finger Puppet Templates (page 163)

White computer paper

Scissors

4 baby socks

Hot glue gun and glue

1. Trace the Finger Puppet Templates onto the white paper and cut them out. Use the permanent markers to trace the Finger Puppet cutouts onto the baby socks, with the bottoms of the finger puppets at the openings of the socks and one side of each template on the folded edge of its sock.

2. Trace the fox tail, bird wings and bunny ear cutouts onto the toes of the socks.

3. Cut through both layers of the socks with the scissors or fabric shears, within the shape outlines. The socks should now be able to open up like a book.

4. Apply hot glue between the layers of the small pieces— the tail, wings and ears—and adhere the layers together.

5. Hot-glue the ends of the tail, wings and ears to the inside of the finger puppets.

6. Apply a thin line of hot glue around the inside top and sides of the finger puppets and adhere the layers together.

7. Draw faces and details with the markers. Put the puppets on your fingers and tell a story to your child!

# ▲ FELT ANIMAL MASKS ▲

Your child can transform into an animal with these felt masks. Put a mask on yourself to show your baby or to join in the fun with your toddler. Play peekaboo, hiding behind a mask and popping out, or sit with your baby in front of a mirror and show them how you can hold the mask in front of their face, then remove it for them to play peekaboo with themselves. Turn these masks into costumes with solid-colored outfits and add them to your dress-up collection for your toddler or preschooler!

Permanent marker

Animal Mask Templates (pages 170–171)

White computer paper

Scissors

8 (9 x 12" [23 x 30-cm]) sheets of soft felt in different colors

Hot glue gun and glue

3½ yards (3.5 m) ribbon

Lighter

1. Trace the Animal Mask Templates onto the white computer paper and cut them out with scissors. With the permanent marker, lightly trace the Animal Mask cutouts onto the felt sheets. Use the scissors to cut the eyes out of the Animal Mask cutouts, then trace the eyes onto the felt masks. Cut along the outlines of the felt masks and cut the eyes out of the masks.

2. Cut the fox's cheeks, duck's bill, owl's feather tufts and bear's muzzle from the Animal Mask cutouts and trace them onto the felt, using whatever colors you prefer. Cut the pieces from the felt sheets.

3. Cut the fox's inner ears, owl's beak and bear's inner ears and nose from the Animal Mask cutouts and trace them onto the felt, using whatever colors you prefer. Cut the pieces from the felt sheets.

4. Apply hot glue to the fox's cheeks, duck's bill, owl's feather tufts, bear's muzzle and inner ears and adhere them to the masks. Be careful and hold the outer edges of the pieces, so that they do not fold as you move them and so that you do not burn your hands. Apply hot glue to the masks and adhere the owl's beak and the bear's nose.

5. Turn the masks over. Cut 8 (16-inch [40-cm]) lengths of ribbon and seal the ends by running them quickly over the flame of a lighter. Hot-glue the ribbons to the back of the masks, one on each side of the mask.

6. Tie the mask around your or your child's face with a bow in the ribbon, and supervise while they play!

# POURING MILK-JUG FISH

This fun bath toy is a great tool for pretend play and learning! Scooping and pouring are important motor skills that can teach your child how to use their eyes and hands simultaneously, and they can also teach early math concepts like less and more. Toss this toy in the bath, a large storage bin or baby pool with water, rubber duckies and plastic cups. Younger babies will like watching you pour water from the fish's mouth and can try putting duckies inside the fish. Older babies and toddlers can scoop up water and pour it into the tub or cups. Use this fish as a sand toy as well for a fun tactile sensory experience.

1 (1-gallon [3.8-L]) milk or water jug

Alcohol pad

Permanent marker

Precision crafting knife

Hot glue gun and glue

2 empty snack pouches

Serrated knife

1. Wash and dry the milk jug, being sure to remove any labels. Use the alcohol pad to remove printed dates from the jug.

2. With the permanent marker, draw a mouth for the fish that looks like a person's lips on the bottom of the milk jug. Cut out the mouth with a precision crafting knife and save the cutout—it will become the tail of the fish.

3. Cut off the pointed top of the mouth shape from the bottom of the jug. Use the precision crafting knife to smooth any rough edges of the hole and the mouth cutout.

4. Trace the jug's lid onto the middle of the mouth cutout, which will become the fish's tail. Cut the circle out of the tail. Any remaining permanent marker can be removed with an alcohol pad.

5. Apply hot glue around the neck of the jug—where the lid would normally twist on—then put the fish's tail over the neck of the jug and hold it in place while the glue dries. Apply hot glue to the inside of the lid, twist the lid onto the jug and allow the glue to set, so that the lid and tail cannot be removed.

6. Cut the necks and lids from each of the snack food pouches with a serrated knife, right above the plastic pouch. Discard the plastic pouches and clean the lids and necks. Allow the lids and necks to dry completely. Trace a pouch's neck onto both sides of the jug to represent the fish's eyes. Cut the circles out with a precision crafting knife.

7. Apply hot glue to the pouch's necks, then push them through the holes so that the threads are pointing out of the holes. Apply hot glue to the inside of the pouch's lids and twist them onto the threads. Throw this toy in the bath for some imaginative scooping fun!

# CAR CUBBYHOLES

Create cubbies for your child's favorite toy cars, animal figurines, peg people or finger puppets. With toilet paper tubes and some imagination, you can create a parking garage, zoo, beehive, apartment building and more. This open-ended toy puts your child in the driver's seat, directing play toward their interests. Painting the rolls can add a color-matching element for toddlers and make the cubbies more appealing. When choosing toys to put in the cubbies, opt for toys that are labeled for babies or that are at least 1¼ inches (3 cm) in diameter if your child is still mouthing. If you would like to fit larger toys into the cubbies, gift wrap tubes are often larger in diameter than toilet paper tubes.

10 toilet paper tubes, 4 paper towel tubes or 2 gift wrap tubes

Scissors (optional)

Paintbrush and acrylic paint in different colors

Hot glue gun and glue

Toys to fit inside the cubbyholes

1. If you are using 10 toilet paper tubes, skip to step 2. If you are using 4 paper towel tubes or 2 gift wrap tubes, cut them into 10 tubes of equal length with the scissors.

2. To quickly paint the rolls, hold 2 fingers up to make the peace sign, and place 1 tube over them. Rotate the roll as you paint, then stand it upright on a table to dry. Paint the rolls any color or pattern you would like.

3. When the paint has fully dried, apply a line of hot glue to about two-thirds of the length of a tube and adhere another tube next to it. Using this method, glue 4 tubes in a diagonal row.

4. Apply hot glue to the concave area on the adhered tubes where the other tubes will rest when they are stacked on top, and adhere another tube on top. Repeat this process until there are 3 tubes staggered on top of the bottom 4 tubes. Use the same method to adhere 2 tubes in a row, and then 1 tube on top.

5. Put out toys for your child to sort into the cubbies. Peg dolls or finger puppets are a great option for babies!

Toilet training can be a lengthy process that involves many steps for your child to learn. Acting the procedure out with a baby doll can be a great way for your child to learn how to lift the toilet lid, sit on the toilet, go potty and wash their hands in a low-pressure, fun way. Dolls are essential toys for all kids; they teach social processing, empathy and more.[19] Setting up invitations to play, like this bathroom, can help boost your child's imagination and encourage independent play.

▲ ▲ ▲

Ruler

Pencil

1 (42-oz [1.2-kg]) oatmeal canister with a plastic snap-on lid

Paintbrush and acrylic paint in 2 colors

Precision crafting knife

Brad paper fastener

Hot glue gun and glue

Cardboard shoebox

Painters' tape or masking tape

1 (8-oz [224-g]) round plastic container (such as a sour cream or cottage cheese container)

Cardboard

Doll

1. With the ruler and pencil, measure and mark a line on the empty, clean oatmeal canister 4 inches (10 cm) upward from the bottom of the canister. Paint the entire area with acrylic paint. If the center of the oatmeal lid is paper, paint the lid as well. When the paint is dry, use a precision crafting knife to cut the canister so that it measures 3 inches (8 cm) tall.

2. Cut a small slit in the rim of the oatmeal lid and near the top of the painted canister with a precision crafting knife. Poke a brad paper fastener through both slits, open the end of the brad and test to see if the lid will open and close. Hot-glue the end of the brad inside the canister so it cannot be removed.

3. With the shoebox lying on one of its long sides, measure 6 inches (15 cm) toward the middle from either the left- or right-hand end of the shoebox. Mark this section. Paint all sides of the 6-inch (15-cm) section of the shoebox with acrylic paint, and once it dries, cut out the section with the precision crafting knife. Add any desired details, like cabinet doors, by taping off those portions with painters' tape. Paint those areas in a different color.

4. Lightly trace the top of a clean round plastic container onto the cardboard shoebox vanity. Cut out the circle slightly smaller than drawn, so that the rim of the plastic container will rest on the "counter." Place the container in the hole to form the sink.

5. To make an optional faucet, cut 1 (1 x 1–inch [2.5 x 2.5–cm]) piece of cardboard and 1 (1 x 2–inch [2.5 x 5–cm]) piece of cardboard. Hot-glue the pieces to form an L shape. Apply hot glue to the 1 x 2–inch (2.5 x 5–cm) piece, then adhere it to the back of the vanity. Set the vanity and toilet out for your child's dolls.

1.

2.

3.

4.

# BREEZY BOTTLE BOAT

Set up boat races or spruce up bath time with these recycled bottle boats. Infants can watch a boat float by in a low dish of water during tummy time—push it along and watch their gaze follow. Babies who are able to sit can push the boat around while they sit in a large storage bin or bathtub. Throw some toy animals in the tub with your child to get their imagination going—the animals can board the boat and sail the high seas. Help your toddler develop oral motor skills and increase muscle tone by making two boats and racing them in a baby pool by blowing their sails. Blowing is a skill that may emerge around two or three years old, and working up to blowing efficiently is great exercise for the jaw and mouth.

Plastic bottle with flat sides

#2 HDPE plastic canister lid measuring at least 4" (10 cm) in diameter (#2 HDPE plastic is soft and can be cut with scissors)

Hot glue gun and glue

Plastic sports drink lid

Standard-sized hot glue stick

Permanent marker

Precision crafting knife

1. Clean a plastic bottle with flat sides. Let it dry completely. Wash and dry the plastic canister lid. Lids from raisin or cocoa powder canisters work well for this project.

2. To make the boat's mast, apply hot glue to the inside of the plastic sports drink lid. Place a standard-sized hot glue stick in the hot glue. Hold the glue stick upright as the hot glue dries.

3. With the permanent marker, draw triangular sails on the plastic canister lid. Cut out the sails with a precision crafting knife.

4. Apply hot glue to the hot glue stick mast, then adhere the plastic sails.

5. Lay the plastic bottle on one of its flat sides. With the precision crafting knife, carefully cut a large rounded or oval hole out of the top of the side facing up. Cut off any jagged pieces so the hole is smooth.

6. Apply hot glue to the inside of the plastic bottle boat and adhere the base of the mast and sail.

7. When the glue is dry, put the boat in a shallow bin or tub of water and let your child explore.

# RHYTHMIC RAINSTICK

Your baby can create the sound of rainfall and participate in a visual and auditory sensory experience with this easy-to-make rainstick. Baby can shake the bottle, roll it, watch the beans move and listen. The contrasting colors of the beans makes this a great focal point for tummy time! Toddlers can experiment with moving the rainstick upright quickly or slowly and shaking it softly or vigorously and listening for the different sounds the rainstick produces. Close your eyes with your child and encourage them to imagine that rain is falling around the two of you as you hear the beans move through the sticks. Involve your little one in creating the sensory bottle as well–take your child outside and let them gather twigs in a basket. Test various fillers with the twigs–like assorted dry beans, rice and popcorn kernels–in multiple bottles with your child and encourage them to observe the differences in sound.

▲   ▲   ▲

15 to 20 small, dry twigs

12- to 20-oz (360- to 600-ml) clear plastic bottle with lid

Funnel

¼ cup (49 g) dried black beans (see step 2)

¼ cup (49 g) dried white beans (see step 2)

Hot glue gun and glue

1. Break the twigs to fit inside the plastic bottle. Include twigs of different heights and with varying curvature.

2. Put the twigs in the bottle, then insert the funnel into the mouth of the bottle. Add the black beans and white beans. You can substitute with other kinds of dried beans, uncooked rice, popcorn kernels, dried split peas or dried lentils.

3. Close the bottle's lid and shake the bottle to distribute the beans. Remove the lid and apply a small amount of hot glue to the inside of the lid, then tighten the lid on the bottle. Allow the glue to set.

4. Let your child make music and watch the beans fall.

# TEMPLATES

Transforming Disks (page 21)

Baby-Sock Finger Puppets (page 148)

Magnetic Fishing (page 29)

Black-and-White Montessori Mobile (page 120)

5

6

7

1

Clothespin Sun and Cloud (page 83)

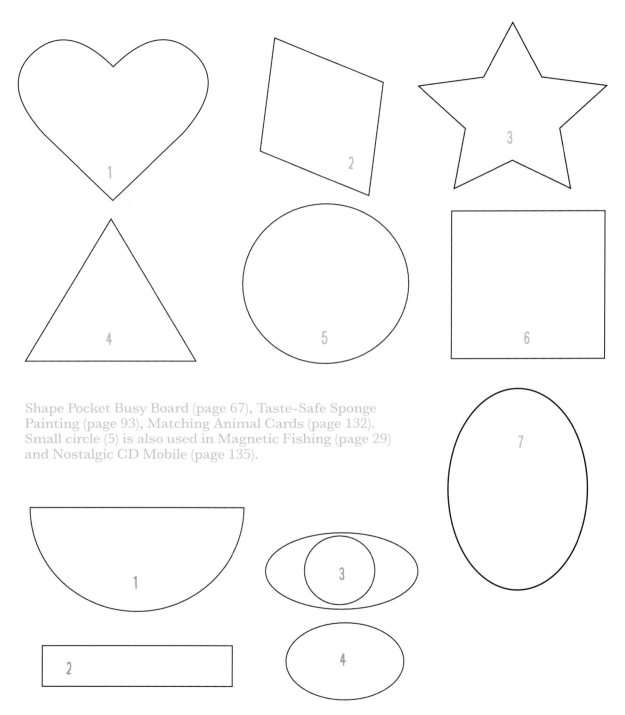

Shape Pocket Busy Board (page 67), Taste-Safe Sponge Painting (page 93), Matching Animal Cards (page 132). Small circle (5) is also used in Magnetic Fishing (page 29) and Nostalgic CD Mobile (page 135).

Emotion-Changing Face (page 115)

Peekaboo Board (page 119)

Make-Believe Mailbox (page 141)

1

1

2

4

3

1

Farm Animal Shadow Puppets (page 123)

Farm Animal Shadow Puppets (page 123)

Matching Animal Cards (page 132)

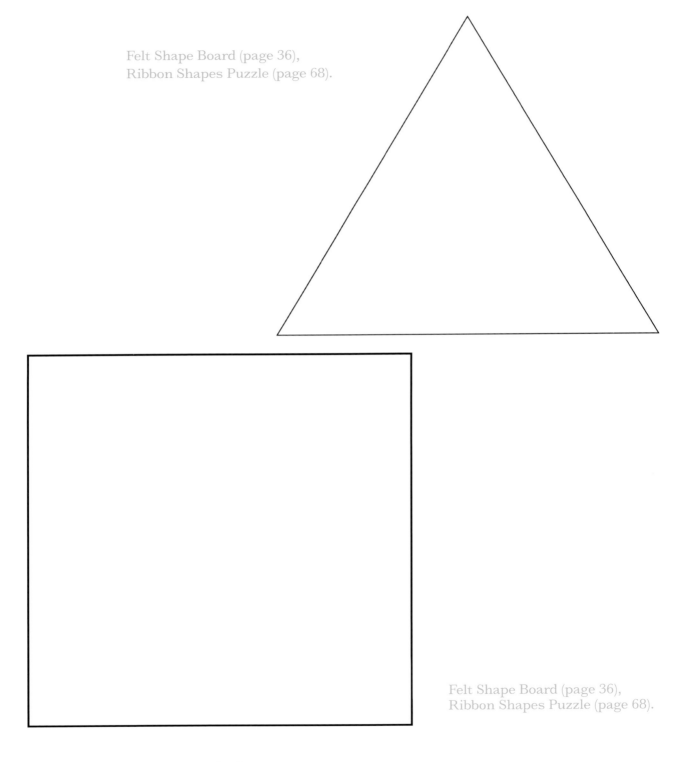

Felt Shape Board (page 36),
Ribbon Shapes Puzzle (page 68).

Felt Shape Board (page 36),
Ribbon Shapes Puzzle (page 68).

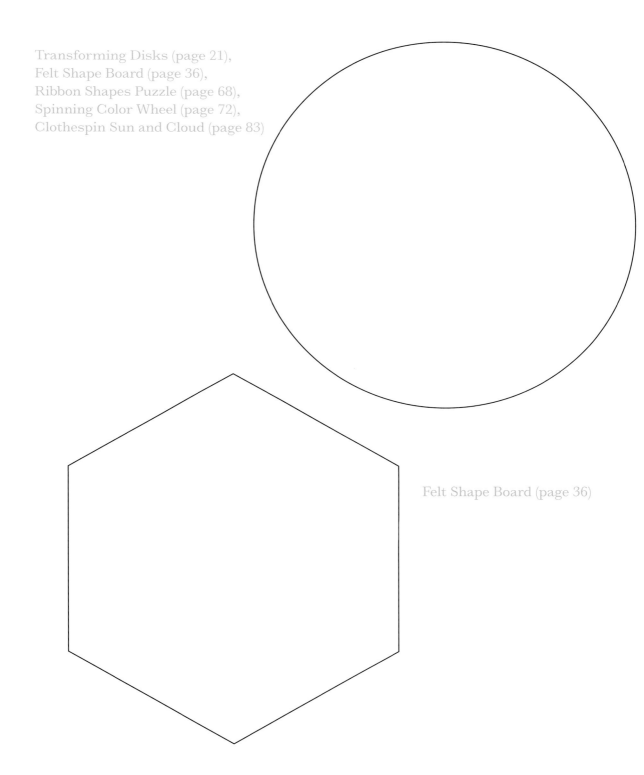

# PROJECT RECOMMENDATIONS BY AGE

Reference the index below for a quick guide to the top projects recommended per age range. This curated list can give you an idea of where to start based on your child's age, and the icons in each project show a wider range for which each project is suitable. You can find suggestions for how to use the projects for different ages and in varying ways in the project descriptions.

# PROJECT INDEX BY SKILL

In the guide below, find projects to try by the skills they develop. Primary skills, noted as PS, are the predominant skills strengthened by the respective activity. Primary skills in bold text are those that are highlighted by the icons at the top of the project pages. Secondary skills, SS, are noted in the index below as well to show other abilities your child can hone with the play ideas. Search for activities by play positions as well: tummy time, back play, seated and standing play.

## CHAPTER 1: STRENGTHENING AND ACTIVE PLAY

|  | Tummy Time | Back Play | Seated Play | Standing Play | Examining | Sorting | Predicting | Communicating | Creating |
|---|---|---|---|---|---|---|---|---|---|
| Tummy Time Stand | PS |  | SS |  | PS |  |  |  | PS |
| Spider Web Toy Grab |  |  | PS |  |  |  |  |  |  |
| Rattle Socks |  | PS |  |  | SS |  |  |  |  |
| Transforming Disks | SS | SS | PS |  | SS |  | SS |  |  |
| Vroom! Vroom! Box Car |  |  | PS | SS |  |  |  | SS | PS |
| Wipeable Car Play Mat |  |  | PS |  |  |  | SS | SS | PS |
| Magnetic Fishing |  |  | PS |  |  |  | SS | SS |  |
| Pound-a-Ball |  |  | SS | PS | SS | SS | SS |  |  |
| Color Cap Match | SS |  | PS | SS |  |  |  |  |  |
| Felt Shape Board | SS |  | SS | PS |  |  |  | PS |  |
| Vibrant Straw Roller | PS |  | SS |  | SS |  |  |  |  |

## CHAPTER 2: INVESTIGATION AND DISCOVERY

|  | Tummy Time | Back Play | Seated Play | Standing Play | Examining | Sorting | Predicting | Communicating | Creating |
|---|---|---|---|---|---|---|---|---|---|
| Family Faces Book | PS |  | SS |  | SS |  |  | PS |  |
| Sliding Surprise Box |  |  | PS |  | SS |  | PS |  |  |
| Jingle Ball Run |  |  |  | PS |  |  | PS |  |  |
| Egg Carton Color Sort |  |  | PS |  |  | PS |  |  |  |
| Lid Stacking Rings |  |  | PS |  |  | SS |  |  |  |
| Pajama Pull | PS |  | SS |  | PS |  |  |  |  |
| Link Drop Box |  |  | PS | SS |  | SS |  |  |  |
| Smiley Cards and Wallet |  |  | PS |  | SS | SS |  | SS |  |
| Pop Drop |  |  |  | PS |  | PS | SS |  |  |
| Shadow Projector Tubes |  |  | SS | PS |  |  |  | PS | SS |
| Hide-and-Find Pouches |  |  | PS |  | SS | PS |  |  |  |

| Discovering | Imagining | Experimenting | Strengthening | Refining | Matching | Grasping | Counting | Seeing | Hearing | Touching |
|---|---|---|---|---|---|---|---|---|---|---|
|  |  |  | PS |  |  |  |  | SS |  |  |
| PS |  | SS | PS | SS |  | PS |  |  |  |  |
| SS |  | PS | PS |  |  |  |  |  | PS |  |
| PS |  | SS | PS |  |  | SS |  | SS |  |  |
|  | SS |  | PS |  |  |  |  |  |  |  |
|  | PS | SS | PS |  |  |  |  |  |  |  |
|  | SS | SS | PS | PS |  |  | PS |  |  |  |
| PS |  | SS | PS | SS |  | SS |  |  | PS |  |
|  |  | SS | PS | PS | PS | SS |  |  |  |  |
|  |  |  | PS | PS |  | SS |  |  |  |  |
|  |  |  | PS |  |  | PS |  |  | PS |  |

| Discovering | Imagining | Experimenting | Strengthening | Refining | Matching | Grasping | Counting | Seeing | Hearing | Touching |
|---|---|---|---|---|---|---|---|---|---|---|
| PS |  |  |  |  |  | SS |  | SS |  | SS |
| PS |  | SS | SS |  |  | SS |  |  |  |  |
| PS |  | PS |  |  |  |  |  | SS | SS |  |
| PS |  |  |  |  | SS | PS | SS |  |  |  |
| PS |  | PS |  | PS |  | SS | SS |  |  |  |
| PS |  |  |  | PS |  | SS |  |  |  | SS |
| PS |  | PS |  | SS |  | SS |  |  |  |  |
| PS | PS |  |  | PS |  | SS |  | SS |  |  |
| PS |  |  | SS |  | SS | SS | PS |  |  |  |
| PS | SS | PS |  | SS |  |  |  | SS |  |  |
| PS |  |  |  | PS | SS |  |  |  |  |  |

| | Tummy Time | Back Play | Seated Play | Standing Play | Examining | Sorting | Predicting | Communicating | Creating |
|---|---|---|---|---|---|---|---|---|---|
| Shape Pocket Busy Board | | | PS | | | | | SS | |
| Ribbon Shapes Puzzle | | | PS | | | | | | |
| Jumbo Rainbow Crayons | | | PS | | | | | | PS |
| Spinning Color Wheel | | | PS | | SS | | | | |
| Smiling Face Puzzle | PS | | SS | | | | SS | | |
| Ring Box Pull | | | PS | SS | | | | SS | |
| Counting Bead Slide | | | PS | | | SS | | | |
| Bat-and-Play Ribbon Octopus | SS | PS | SS | | SS | | | SS | |
| Clothespin Sun and Cloud | | | PS | | | PS | | SS | |
| Pouch Lid Tracks | | | PS | | | | | | |
| Drop-and-Twist Station | | | PS | | | SS | | | |
| Ribbon Colander | PS | | SS | | | | | | |

| | Tummy Time | Back Play | Seated Play | Standing Play | Examining | Sorting | Predicting | Communicating | Creating |
|---|---|---|---|---|---|---|---|---|---|
| Taste-Safe Sponge Painting | | | PS | | | | | | PS |
| Tube Shakers | | PS | | | | | | | |
| Crinkle Square | SS | PS | SS | | | | | | |
| Ocean Bottle | PS | | | | PS | | SS | | |
| Button Water Mat | PS | | SS | | PS | | | | |
| Rainbow Chickpea Shaker | PS | | SS | | SS | | | | |
| Tactile Sensory Path | SS | | SS | PS | | | PS | | |
| Bead Squishy Bag | PS | | SS | SS | SS | | | | |
| Cake Tin Drum | PS | | SS | SS | | | | | |
| Natural Sensory Lids | PS | | SS | | PS | | | | |

| Discovering | Imagining | Experimenting | Strengthening | Refining | Matching | Grasping | Counting | Seeing | Hearing | Touching |
|---|---|---|---|---|---|---|---|---|---|---|
| SS | | SS | | PS | PS | | | | | SS |
| | | SS | | PS | PS | PS | | | | |
| | | | SS | PS | | PS | | | | |
| | | SS | | PS | PS | | | SS | | |
| PS | | | | PS | | PS | | SS | | |
| SS | | | PS | PS | | PS | | | | |
| | | | | PS | | SS | PS | | | |
| | SS | | | PS | | PS | | PS | | |
| | SS | | | PS | SS | PS | SS | | | |
| | PS | | | PS | | SS | | | | |
| | | PS | | PS | | SS | SS | | | |
| | | PS | SS | PS | | SS | | SS | | |

| Discovering | Imagining | Experimenting | Strengthening | Refining | Matching | Grasping | Counting | Seeing | Hearing | Touching |
|---|---|---|---|---|---|---|---|---|---|---|
| | | SS | | PS | | SS | | | | PS |
| | | | | | | PS | | | PS | |
| | | | | | | SS | | | PS | PS |
| PS | SS | SS | | | | SS | | PS | | |
| | | SS | SS | | | | | SS | | PS |
| | | | SS | | | PS | | SS | PS | |
| PS | | SS | SS | | | | | | | PS |
| | | | SS | PS | | | | SS | | PS |
| | | SS | SS | PS | | | | | PS | |
| SS | | | | | | | | SS | | PS |

## CHAPTER 5: VISUAL EXPLORATION

| | Tummy Time | Back Play | Seated Play | Standing Play | Examining | Sorting | Predicting | Communicating | Creating |
|---|---|---|---|---|---|---|---|---|---|
| Emotion-Changing Face | SS | | PS | | | | | PS | SS |
| "I Spy" Bottle | SS | | PS | | SS | | | PS | |
| Peekaboo Board | SS | | PS | | | | SS | SS | |
| Black-and-White Montessori Mobile | SS | PS | | | PS | | | | |
| Farm Animal Shadow Puppets | | | SS | PS | | | | PS | |
| Colorful Pom-Pom Garlands | | PS | | | PS | | | | |
| Rainbow Spinner | SS | PS | SS | | | | | | |
| Playing Card Gallery | SS | | PS | | PS | | | | |
| Nature Mobile | | PS | | | PS | | | | |
| Matching Animal Cards | | | PS | | | PS | SS | SS | |
| Nostalgic CD Mobile | SS | PS | | | PS | | | | |

## CHAPTER 6: IMAGINATIVE AND DRAMATIC PLAY

| | Tummy Time | Back Play | Seated Play | Standing Play | Examining | Sorting | Predicting | Communicating | Creating |
|---|---|---|---|---|---|---|---|---|---|
| Squashy Sock Bunnies | SS | SS | PS | | | | | | |
| Make-Believe Mailbox | | | SS | PS | | | | PS | SS |
| Superb Doll Swing | | | | PS | | | | PS | |
| Baby-Sock Finger Puppets | | | PS | | | | PS | PS | |
| Felt Animal Masks | | | SS | PS | | | | PS | |
| Pouring Milk-Jug Fish | | | PS | SS | | | SS | | |
| Car Cubbyholes | | | PS | | | PS | | | |
| Baby Doll Bathroom | | | PS | | | | | PS | |
| Breezy Bottle Boat | SS | | PS | | | | PS | SS | |
| Rhythmic Rainstick | PS | | SS | | SS | | | | |

| Discovering | Imagining | Experimenting | Strengthening | Refining | Matching | Grasping | Counting | Seeing | Hearing | Touching |
|---|---|---|---|---|---|---|---|---|---|---|
|  | SS | SS |  | PS |  |  |  | PS |  |  |
| PS |  |  |  |  |  | SS |  | PS |  |  |
| PS |  |  |  | PS |  |  |  | PS |  | SS |
|  |  |  | PS |  |  |  |  | PS |  |  |
| SS | PS | SS |  |  |  | SS |  | PS |  |  |
|  |  |  | PS |  |  |  |  | PS |  |  |
| SS |  |  | PS | PS |  |  |  | PS |  |  |
|  |  |  | PS | SS |  |  |  | PS |  |  |
| PS |  |  |  |  |  |  |  | PS |  |  |
|  |  |  |  |  | PS |  | SS | PS |  |  |
| PS |  |  |  |  |  |  |  | PS |  |  |

| Discovering | Imagining | Experimenting | Strengthening | Refining | Matching | Grasping | Counting | Seeing | Hearing | Touching |
|---|---|---|---|---|---|---|---|---|---|---|
| PS | PS |  |  |  |  | PS |  |  |  | SS |
| PS | PS |  |  | SS |  |  |  |  |  |  |
|  | PS | SS | PS |  |  |  |  |  |  |  |
|  | PS |  |  | SS |  |  |  |  |  |  |
| PS | PS |  |  |  |  |  |  |  |  |  |
|  | PS | PS | PS |  |  | SS |  |  |  |  |
| PS | PS |  |  | SS | SS |  | SS |  |  |  |
| PS | PS |  |  |  |  |  |  |  |  |  |
|  | PS | PS |  |  |  |  |  |  |  |  |
| SS | PS | SS | SS |  |  | PS |  |  | PS |  |

# ATTRIBUTIONS

1. Dauch, C., Imwalle, M., Ocasio, B., & Metz, A. E. (2018). The influence of the number of toys in the environment on toddlers' play. Infant Behavior and Development, 50, 78–87. 10.1016/j.infbeh.2017.11.005

2. Levin, D. E., & Rosenquest, B. (2001). The increasing role of electronic toys in the lives of infants and toddlers: Should we be concerned? Contemporary Issues in Early Childhood, 2(2), 242–247. https://doi.org/10.2304/ciec.2001.2.2.9

3. Yogman, M., Garner, A., Hutchinson, J., Hirsh-Pasek, K., Michnick Golinkoff, R., & Committee on Psychosocial Aspects of Child and Family Health, & Council on Communications and Media. (2018). The power of play: A pediatric role in enhancing development in young children. Pediatrics, 142(3), 2018–2058. https://doi.org/10.1542/peds.

4. American Academy of Pediatrics. (2009, August 1). Cognitive development: 8 to 12 months. Healthy Children. https://www.healthychildren.org/English/ages-stages/baby/Pages/Cognitive-Development-8-to-12-Months.aspx

5. Gaertner, B. M., Spinrad, T. L., & Eisenberg, N. (2008). Focused attention in toddlers: measurement, stability, and relations to negative emotion and parenting. Infant and child development, 17(4), 339–363. https://doi.org/10.1002/ICD.580

6. Schwartz, K. (2015, March 26). Why kids need to move, touch and experience to learn. Retrieved from https://www.kqed.org/mindshift/39684/why-kids-need-to-move-touch-and-experience-to-learn

7. Campbell, J. (2016, November 14). Why crawling is important for your baby [Web log post]. Retrieved from https://www.nationwidechildrens.org/family-resources-education/700childrens/2016/11/why-crawling-is-important-for-your-baby

8. U.S. Department of Health and Human Services (n.d.). Babies need tummy time! National Institute of Child Health and Human Development. Retrieved from https://safetosleep.nichd.nih.gov/safesleepbasics/tummytime

9. Baby Begin. (n.d.). Let's get to know tummy time. Retrieved from https://babybegin.com/tummy-time

10. Adolph, K. E., & Franchak, J. M. (2017). The development of motor behavior. WIREs Cognitive Science, 8(1–2). 10.1002/wcs.1430. https://doi.org/10.1002/wcs.1430

11. Mosaic Rehabilitation. (n.d.). Gross motor milestone series: Kneeling. Retrieved from https://mosaicrehabmt.com/gross-motor-milestone-series-kneeling/

12. Yakimishyn, J. E., & Magill-Evans, J. (2002). Comparisons among tools, surface orientation, and pencil grasp for children 23 months of age. American Journal of Occupational Therapy, 56(5), 564–572. https://doi.org/10.5014/ajot.56.5.564

13. Kaufman, S. B., Singer, J. L., & Singer, D. G. (2012, March 6). The need for pretend play in child development. https://www.psychologytoday.com/us/blog/beautiful-minds/201203/the-need-pretend-play-in-child-development

14. Farzin, F., Hou, C., & Norcia, A. M. (2012). Piecing it together: Infants' neural responses to face and object structure. Journal of Vision, 12(13), 6. https://doi.org/10.1167/12.13.6

15. Goodstart Early Learning. (2018, March 12). Exploring the benefits of sensory play. Retrieved from https://www.goodstart.org.au/news-and-advice/october-2016/exploring-the-benefits-of-sensory-play

16. Pathways.org. (n.d.). Sensory. Retrieved from https://pathways.org/topics-of-development/sensory/#0

17. American Optometric Association. (n.d.). Infant vision: Birth to 24 months of age. Retrieved from https://www.aoa.org/healthy-eyes/eye-health-for-life/infant-vision?sso=y

18. Johnson, S. P. (2010). How infants learn about the visual world. Cognitive Science, 34(7), 1158–1184. https://doi.org/10.1111/j.1551-6709.2010.01127.x

19. Hashmi, S., Vanderwert, R. E., Price, H. A., & Gerson, S. A. (2020). Exploring the benefits of doll play through neuroscience. Frontiers in Human Neuroscience, 14, 413. https://doi.org/10.3389/fnhum.2020.560176

# ACKNOWLEDGMENTS

I have to begin by sincerely thanking my community of friends and followers for engaging with and sharing my work.

I could not have written this book without my father and agent, Greg Daniel, who not only raised me to love reading, writing and artistic pursuits but also inspired and encouraged me to write this book. Your support has been priceless.

Thank you to my mom, Karen, for being my thrifty inspiration—my childhood of playing with aluminum foil doll outfits, buttons and homemade play dough is a huge part of my creative influence.

I am eternally grateful for my husband, Mohssen, who is not only an incredible partner and father but who is also always there to offer engineering and creative advice for all my crafts, as well as a fresh perspective on my photos and writing.

Thank you to the Page Street Publishing team—specifically Caitlin Dow, Rosie Stewart, Meg Baskis, Sarah Monroe and Laura Benton—for making this book a reality.

Finally, thank you to my wonderful children for being my models and motivation, and to all the precious kids who are featured in my photographs.

# ABOUT THE AUTHOR

Hannah Fathi is a thrifty mother of two and architect whose blog, Instagram and phone and web application, Baby Play Hacks, is known for inventive, inexpensive ideas for baby and toddler play.

Hannah's creativity, resourcefulness and love of play and learning are the foundation for her content and community, and her goal is to give parents and caregivers ideas that are practical and frugal. Hannah and her husband's company, Little Light LLC, creates useful tools for early childhood and beyond, and Hannah's work on Baby Play Hacks has been featured in online media, including Babylist and *Good Housekeeping*.

Hannah lives with her daughter, son and husband in the San Francisco Bay Area. When she isn't chasing after her children, singing nursery rhymes or creating baby activities, Hannah dabbles in various creative pursuits like drawing, embroidery and writing.

# INDEX